Pastoral Care for Lay People

Pastoral Care for Lay People

FRANK WRIGHT

SCM PRESS LTD

√ 334 02240 1

First published 1982
by SCM Press Ltd
58 Bloomsbury Street, London

Typeset by Gloucester Typesetting Services
and printed in Great Britain by
Richard Clay (The Chaucer Press) Ltd
Bungay, Suffolk

Contents

Foreword

This book is addressed directly to lay people, so an apology is due straight away. I am yet another clergyman writing such a book, open to the charge of clerical patronizing and of not taking seriously the proper and distinct vocation of the lay person. But my work, I trust, prevents such an attitude, since I am alongside secular colleagues, in a university extra-mural department, teaching religious, and especially pastoral, studies. This has given me many opportunities over the past fifteen years to listen to lay people with very different backgrounds and to share in their struggles in local churches. This book is a fruit of that experience, and if any dedication were necessary, it would be to those who have shared their reflections with me, and from whom I have learnt much.

I have to say, too, that it seems as if so far there has been little considered analysis, either by clerics or lay people, of what lay pastoral care is, and could be. Analysis describes something of my aim, but the word is too clinical. I am here simply trying to paint one picture of lay pastoral care today, to encourage further reflection by individuals and discussion by church groups. It is an impressionistic picture, and does not portray every area of lay experience. It tries to catch the spirit without imprisoning it, so it is not a book which tries to explain 'how to do it', or give instructions, as a motor-car manual might do. To attempt that would not only be arrogant; it would fail to do justice to the rich variety of person we meet and the different situations in which we are placed, and could not possibly catch or describe the sensitivity which pastoral care demands.

To paint a picture is to appeal to the imagination, to show things in a different light, to stretch the horizon of possibilities: that is my hope for this book.

To avoid ugliness and the weariness of repetition, I have used 'he' when 'he and/or she' is genuinely meant; and I have deliberately kept quotations and footnotes to the minimum. I have, however, made one or two suggestions at the end of the book for further reading and study for those who wish to explore any questions and issues raised at greater depth.

I

Why Pastoral Care?

A modern parable recalls us sharply to a proper sense of priorities in the church.

On a dangerous seacoast where shipwrecks often occur there was once a crude little lifesaving station. The building was just a hut, and there was only one boat, but the few devoted members kept a constant watch over the sea, and with no thought for themselves went out day and night tirelessly searching for the lost. Many lives were saved by this wonderful little station, so that it became famous. Some of those who were saved, and various others in the surrounding area, wanted to become associated with the station and give of their time and money and effort for the support of its work. New boats were bought and new crews trained. The little lifesaving station grew.

Some of the members of the lifesaving station were unhappy that the building was so crude and poorly equipped. They felt that a more comfortable place should be provided as the first refuge of those saved from the sea. So they replaced the emergency cots with beds and put better furniture in the enlarged building. Now the lifesaving station became a popular gathering place for its members, and they decorated it beautifully and furnished it exquisitely, because they used it as a sort of club. Fewer members were now interested in going to sea on lifesaving missions, so they hired lifeboat crews to do this work. The lifesaving motif still prevailed in the club's decoration, and there was a liturgical lifeboat in the room where the club initiations were held. About this time a large ship was wrecked off the coast, and the hired crews brought in boatloads of cold, wet and half-drowned people. They were dirty and sick, and some of them had black skin and some had yellow skin. The beautiful new club was in chaos. So the property committee immediately had a shower house built outside the club where victims of shipwreck could be cleaned up before coming inside.

At the next meeting, there was a split in the club membership. Most of the members wanted to stop the club's lifesaving activities as being unpleasant and a hindrance to the normal social life of the club. Some members insisted upon lifesaving as their primary purpose and pointed out that they were still called a lifesaving station. But they were finally voted down and told that if they wanted to save the lives of all the various kinds of people who were shipwrecked in those waters, they could begin their own lifesaving station down the coast. They did.

As the years went by, the new station experienced the same changes that had occurred in the old. It evolved into a club, and yet another lifesaving station was founded. History continued to repeat itself, and if you visit that sea coast today, you will find a number of exclusive clubs along that shore. Shipwrecks are frequent in those waters, but most of the people drown![1]

However well-ordered and attractive a church may seem, unless it is seeking to answer the deepest needs which people experience, then it is largely irrelevant. That is why pastoral care must be at the heart of the church's life.

But there is a strange irony. Clergymen and ministers have traditionally been seen as those who exercise pastoral care, those who shepherd people through the changes and chances of this mortal life. That is felt to be a major part of their professional task; they have been trained for it, and it is a task well understood often by those with tenuous connections ('The vicar never came to see us once when my husband was dying of cancer . . .'). In practice, lay people, unsung and often even unnoticed, have often been and still are those who exercise pastoral care in the shape of kindness. The husband dying of cancer may not have been visited by the vicar, but almost certainly some church person in the road will have offered some practical help. That spontaneous lay caring is heart-warming. Nothing that this book attempts to do by way of exploring a more effective total lay caring should rob it of its spontaneity. Nor must I give the impression that I am suggesting an order of 'auxiliary professionals', for whom training and the development of techniques are essential. But there are certain questions to be asked; and the most basic is, 'Why pastoral care at all?'

However gloomy and despressing the picture of modern life, the un-selfconscious acts of pastoral care which, of course, are not confined to church people, have their roots deep in the recognition of human interdependence, in man's instinct for community, his simple humanity. Horrifying stories of injured people left by the roadside as people pass by on the other side, and old people isolated for weeks and weeks in multi-storey blocks of flats, must always be balanced by those innumerable quiet acts of pastoral love and care which may or may not have been explicitly inspired by Christian love, the love of God-in-Christ. The continuing support given to a colleague in the office when he or she is going through a divorce; the readiness to listen to the story of an acquaintance's depression: the list is endless. In a Lancashire town a regular round of refuse collectors exchanged cheery words every week with the old ladies who inhabited a block of flats. When the round was changed, the ladies felt bereft. 'No one *cares* about us now,' they said.

Pastoral care, then, is rooted in human life, and can never be isolated as a professional or even especially spiritual or religious preserve. Indeed, we exercise better care by creating links with the rest of society rather than by separating people and care into special compartments. Self-consciousness or any attempt to make care 'special' diminishes its quality. But since caring and

Christianity seem inseparable, and since pastoral care forms
such a large part of the Christian tradition, we need to ask not
so much what is *distinctive*, as if that were the all-important
question, but what it is that motivates us as Christians. How do
we place our caring in the Christian context?

> Christian faith has its origin in *gratitude*: it is a *response*. What
the Christian has seen, even if it is only in a glimpse, is something of the love that lies eternally in the heart of God. God *is*
love. The Christian believes that he sees that love at work,
partly through God's gifts in his creation and chiefly in Jesus
Christ, whose words and whose deeds are the incarnation of
that love. He earths God's love in human experience. So, having seen, and believing that he has experienced something of
that love, the Christian knows he is a loved creature; loved
unconditionally, and not only when he conforms, or even only
when he repents or, as has often been implied, when he forgives.
The Christian is committed to the statement 'God is love', and
that implies that love is the strongest force in the world. If God
is Almighty God, then his purposes cannot finally be defeated,
and those purposes can only be achieved through the exercise
of love. It has been argued that when we call God Almighty, we
are not describing a power who can, if he so wishes, turn the
Taj Mahal into St Paul's Cathedral, but somehow manages to
restrain himself. We are making an affirmation about the ultimate victory of love over every sin and evil that would *seem* to
defeat it. There is a power in love greater than any sort of
power you could ever mention. Take a very simple and obvious
illustration. Imagine, for a moment, that you are completely
under my thumb, in my control, and that I have a picture of the
sort of person I want you to become. Now I can set about the
business of bringing about that picture in one of two ways: I
can try to watch over you and make you conform in every
detail, by sheer, brute physical force. Or I can use my power in
the sense only of persuasiveness, attractiveness, allowing you,
that is, to have a vision of the person you are to become, and
leaving you completely free to make your own response to it,

knowing that however long it takes, your response is certain. There are only two forms of power where human beings are concerned: coercive power or the power of persuasive love. As a famous philosopher and mathematician said, much earlier this century, it is because we are unconvinced of the power of persuasive love that we want to invest God with dictatorial, coercive power. Of that love, the crucifixion is the supreme illustration, and the force the crucifixion has exercised on the hearts and wills and imaginations of people of different genera- tions is a strong witness. Caesars come and go, but Jesus Christ is the same yesterday, today, and for ever.

The Christian, then, responds in gratitude to God's love: as the New Testament puts it, 'We love, because he loved us first.'[2] It means in practice that he will be seeking all the time to reflect to others that same unconditional love with which he believes he is loved of God, and that experience of another person's unconditional love might be his best chance – humanly speak- ing, his only chance – of coming to know something of God's love. George Herbert, seventeenth-century poet and hymn- writer, expresses this truth beautifully in his poem *Discipline*:

> Then let wrath remove,
> Love will do the deed;
>   For with love
> Stony hearts will bleed.

> Love is swift of foot;
> Love's a man of war,
>   And can shoot,
> And can hit from far.

> Who can scape his bow?
> That which wrought on Thee,
>   Brought Thee low,
> Needs must work on me.

Throw away Thy rod:
Though man frailties hath,
　　　Thou art God:
Throw away Thy wrath.[3]

That attitude of unconditional love, responding to, reflecting
the love of God, will move the Christian to a *continuing* attitude
of care for others: and in that sense, it will become as 'natural'
for him to exercise pastoral care as it will be for him to breathe.

Let me earth that theological exploration in a true story from
a parish I served. We had a group of about twenty-four people
who volunteered to be ready to help in any emergency. They
didn't advertise or call themselves Good Samaritans or anything
like that. But if I or any member of the congregation discovered
anyone in need, there they were – available. And it was one
person's job, at the end of a phone, to match the person with the
need. The Social Services Department in the Town Hall found
it useful, too, to have resources they could call on when the need
didn't fall within any well-defined category. I recall the time
when one lady in her fifties in the parish – we'll call her Mrs
Smith – fell victim to cancer, but was unwilling to go to hospital.
Her husband's work took him away from home on occasions,
and in order to provide day-to-day care, this group of volun-
teers took it upon themselves to organize a rota of helpers.
Whenever I went to visit the patient, I never knew which member of the parish was going to open the door to me. They kept
their rota going for something like six weeks till Mrs Smith died.
And then quietly they withdrew. Now Mrs Smith wasn't a good
churchgoer. She was the daughter of a churchwarden who was
very good at pestering his friends and acquaintances to give
money to the church, and both she and her husband had seen
the church as a grabbing organization, a rather hard-faced
institution. I'll never forget Mr Smith at the graveside. As soon
as the service was over, he said to me how grateful he was to the
people who had looked after his wife, and added, 'I never knew
the church could be like that.' He'd undergone a revolution in

the way he thought about it – not *grabbing*, but *self-giving*. No
amount of talking would have convinced him, but caring in
that sort of situation had made him think again. The caring
wasn't done to impress him or convert him – simply for its own
sake – and the result wasn't that Mr Smith came rushing to
church every Sunday. As a matter of fact, he himself died two
years later. But he had come to see that the church exists like
her Lord, for the sake of those who are in need. It is simply to
be there, loving people just as they are, reflecting the love of
God for each one he has made in his image.

So the inspiration of pastoral care, corporately in the church,
as for the individual Christian, is gratitude for that love that has
been experienced. That of itself tells us little of its nature.
Christians don't need telling that they must love their neighbours because they first love God. Constant exhortation isn't
only counter-productive: it fails to answer important questions,
and in this case the question, 'How?' And to care must be to
love with the mind as well as with the heart. It is to be ready to
exercise all our faculties for the sake of others, ready to think
hard about their needs, imaginatively to put ourselves in their
position, and see things as they see them. And that, in turn,
means being ready to learn about human beings and their needs
from other sources than Christian faith itself. I was brought up
as a Christian to distrust subjects like psychology on the grounds
that they would undermine my Christian faith if I took them
too far. I have now come to see such subjects neither as enemies
nor as allies, but rather, as sources of illumination about man
and his relationships, his hidden fears and guilts, his goals and
ambitions, which we need to ponder if we are going to be able
to help each other as we should, love each other with the mind.
And if we are as alive and alert as we should be as Christians,
we shall be trying to put the pieces of the jigsaw together, seeing
where Christians and others are saying something important
about the same things, even if they're using different language
to do it. Where they appear to be saying different things, then
that only means going on searching until further light dawns.

Our way of caring can be transformed, made much more effective, by discovering for instance, what psychiatrists like Jack Dominian have to say about depression[4] or doctors like Colin Murray Parkes have to say about bereavement.[5]

Pastoral care, then, takes seriously insights from various disciplines about people and caring, integrates head and heart, but can still be imaginative and flexible, since the carer will know that there is more of truth still to be discovered, and what he attempts to do will be provisional in many cases rather than final.

There are severely practical reasons, too, why lay pastoral care is assuming greater importance. Today, we have largely moved away from the idea that the parson was the carer and the laity the cared for, and most parsons could testify to the way in which they have been cared for by the laity – and sometimes spoilt! We can also see now how iniquitous was the assumption that the laity are simply there to do the practical, and sometimes rather tedious, jobs about the church that an overworked parson couldn't find time to do – or didn't want to! The image of the good lay person can easily degenerate into the image of the good *functionary*: the busier he or she is, the better the church person. Of course, there are lay people who express their caring in their doing of practical jobs around the church. But the stripping-down of the church to the bare essentials, demanded by today's world, gives us better opportunity than ever before to see the churches as communities of carers. Moreover, one form of pastoral care, whether it be clerical or lay, will not be superior to another. A *Church Times* reviewer recently seriously suggested that the correct analogy in pastoral care is between Jesus and the parish priest, and between the apostles and the lay people.[6] The implications of such clerical arrogance are devastating: are there not occasions when all of us, priests and laity alike, often resemble Peter in his frailty?

What above all is necessary is that the body of carers which is the church should work out together and with imagination the needs in the community towards the satisfaction of which it can make a useful contribution. Each locality will have something of the same needs, but in some there will be better statutory provision and so on. Isn't this the task of each church, to be looking for ways in which it can care in the community, rather than providing cosiness for its own members? The church's pastoral care goes beyond the business of oiling the wheels institutionally, or helping its members build bridges over temporary difficulty or sickness. This emphasis, rather than the feverish activity to 'keep things going', will paradoxically ensure the survival of the church as a corporate body. Indeed, there is a real sense in which that survival must not be our concern; for the church will find its true self in losing its own self.

The other day, I made one of my infrequent visits to a butcher's shop, and there experienced quite a considerable human feat. Two assistants were discussing their wages as I walked into the otherwise empty shop. They ignored my presence for a moment or two and continued their grumbling. (I was reminded of the cartoon of a would-be customer in a similar situation saying to the two assistants, 'I don't actually mind not being served, but do you think I might just be included in the conversation?') Without even glancing at me once, one of the assistants grunted a 'Yes?', and as he prepared my chop, continued his conversation with his mate. The chop was wrapped, the money paid, and I came out of the shop without our two faces or eyes ever meeting. There's a vignette of modern life, I thought, in which we escape from involvement with each other, treat that delicate and mysterious organism which is the human person, with indifference, if not contempt.

Emphasis on lay pastoral care isn't merely a domestic concern for the Christian and the church. It has many implications, and possible consequences for the wider life of society as a whole. In a world of dehumanizing tendencies we are asserting the unique value of the person in all his or her many-sidedness, and especially in the matter of relationships. In our structured society, which continually emphasizes the need for labels and categories, we are maintaining that the way individuals act, care and are is still significant. We are affirming that each person has his own destiny, which is to discover a Father's heart in that eternal love which is God.

2

Human Needs and Our Response

Before we look further at what pastoral care is, we need to look
at ourselves and our needs. If we are going to experience ourselves as full human beings, what needs must be satisfied? In so
far as exercising pastoral care is using our imagination to try to
answer others' needs (and incidentally, perhaps, our own), we
need to take account of the full range of those needs. Much
misery and frustration, and worse, many neuroses, arise because
we often limit need to the more obvious and easily visible: to
take an example, what else ought we to worry about, goes the
common saying, if we have food in our stomachs and a roof over
our heads?

A model which helps us to consider those needs has been
given us by the psychologist Abraham Maslow, in what has
become known as the 'hierarchy of human needs'.[1] The satisfaction of one need leads to the emergence of the next. First,
there are our *physiological* needs, the need to be fed. Then there
are our *safety* or *security* needs: the need to be able to live and
work against a background of stability and an ordered world.
As we travel further up the scale, our needs become more inter-
nal, relating more and more to our affections and emotions. So
the next need is the need to *belong*. We all need to be able to feel
at home in the company of a group (however small) of friends.
If this need is supplied, then there emerge what Maslow calls
our '*esteem*' needs, the need for a proper self-respect and for the
respect of other people. And finally, there comes the need for
what he calls '*self-actualization*', 'to become everything that one
is capable of becoming'. So Maslow's view is that there are these

five levels of need: physiological, security, belonging, esteem and self-actualization. We need to look more closely at each level, to see how imaginative pastoral caring takes account of these needs, and could attempt to make a contribution to answering them.

Perhaps we're less likely to fail to respond to obvious physiological needs than any other. Satiated as we may be by appeals from relief organizations to help starving people the world over, we can't help being moved by those who are suffering from extreme hunger. In this case, it's easy to take Maslow's point about the appearance of more needs only when other needs have first been satisfied. Pope Paul VI in a papal encyclical stated that man must *know* something and *have* something in order to *be* something. There is, in other words, a minimal subsistence-line below which a person must not be allowed to go if he is going to retain the dignity of being human. We sometimes put 'having' and 'being' in opposition to each other, but sometimes they are complementary. Ascetics can point to the spiritual benefits of fasting; hunger-strikers may be sustained by their passionate convictions; but to be consistently hungry often means a preoccupation with food which excludes all other preoccupations. The desire to eat becomes obsessive. I recall the sight of Russian prisoners-of-war in Germany, prepared to tear each other limb from limb to win the prize of a few potato peelings rescued from the dustbin. William Golding's novel, *Lord of the Flies*, illustrates how once both the constraints of civilization and food-resources are removed, decent respectable people can come close to cannibalism. Hunger, voluntarily undertaken, may be spiritually beneficial; hunger imposed either by an enemy or by circumstances can degrade and de-humanize. Jesus in the Gospels seems to have had experience in himself and others of both sorts of hunger. He fasted and assumed that his disciples would fast: '*When* ye fast,' he said. But his injunction to give Jairus's daughter something to eat, and the feeding of the five thousand, indicate how well he understood man's need for bread.

Perhaps the familiar and crude statistic, that two-thirds of the world's population goes to bed hungry, should always prick our caring conscience and never easily allow us to rest. There may be no obvious evidence of real hunger around us, though what is known as the 'poverty trap' catches more people in this country than we might imagine. But pastoral carers are bound to be ready to take initiatives in world development, and use political influence to ensure a more equitable sharing of the world's resources.

When bodily needs are satisfied, *security* needs become dominant. This need for relative freedom from fear or anxiety is the condition of most healthy living. We assume, even in this increasingly violent society, that we shall be able to go about our daily business without thinking twice as to whether we shall be mugged or coshed or mown down by machine-gun bullets. Again, as with hunger, unless our safety needs are met to some degree, then the desire to meet those needs becomes obsessive. A pensioner in Liverpool, whose flat on the twenty-third storey of a council block has been twice vandalized and herself beaten up, is unlikely to be ready to open the door to anyone or move beyond the threshold. She will be a prisoner, obsessed by her own fears and by the threats that anything outside herself poses to her. This situation, and that generally posed by the urban riots of the early 1980s, points again to the social and political dimension of pastoral care. Beyond anything that the individual may do by way of befriending, there is a necessary task of asking awkward questions at political level about the way architects and planners design boxes on top of each other in which human beings exist; I can hardly say *live*. (Have you ever wondered, as I do every day I pass them on my way from my privileged home, why on earth there isn't more mental instability in a society which forces people to inhabit the dwellings they do?) Of course, feeling insecure takes many forms apart from that of physical safety. My job may be insecure, I may feel I am barely going to be able to provide for my family, my frail health may let me down. It seems as if many fears we knew in childhood carry over into our adult lives, and that better though we are at handling them, they still never really disappear. And there hangs over all of us the black cloud of nuclear war, threatening to mock all our other safety needs. There is clearly an uneasy balance between the safeguarding of our minimal safety needs and living with essential insecurities. What does it mean when we say that the Christian's final security is God, and therefore he should be ready to take risks?

The stark reality which the nuclear threat poses to our safety indicates that there is no final security but in God. Prudent though we must be, we cannot, in the end, make ourselves safe from all the possibilities of harm in the world. Christian faith looks on the blackest of possibilities, even nuclear devastation, and still has to say that nothing will finally separate us from God's love. It is the task of pastoral carers to convey that ultimate assurance; but it is also, for that reason, their task not to allow us to be over-preoccupied with our lesser safety needs. The gospel is about the business of going out not knowing where we're going, of casting our bread on the waters, of not burying our talent lest we lose it. Taking risks is at its heart, because God and his love can never be vanquished. As Julian of Norwich pointed out a long time ago, we are not promised immunity from the world's ills: we are promised that we shall not be overcome – and that, because God is who he is.

In a relatively affluent society, it is perhaps the frustrating of our '*belonging*' needs, the unhappiness of our personal relationships, which causes more frustration than any other. But the word to *belong* needs looking at. 'I need you in order to be myself' is an appropriate piece of shorthand for saying that properly to find ourselves, we need to lose our tightly-knit individual lives in the company of others and in the *close* company of a few. Sometimes we confuse *belonging* and *joining*. Christians often feel that they must be in the *joining* business: that, rather like a jolly aunt at a children's party, the church must get everybody involved, and play the game together. But it's the sensitive child who rebels, and matiness isn't the goal of all our striving. Have we not sometimes frozen out of church life those who didn't express themselves in this way? The Parish Communion Movement, valuable though it has been, has sometimes given the impression that first-class Christians are to be found at *that* service, and those who prefer the quieter, older, more contemplative service are second-class.

My experience tells me that the world is full of people desperate not to *join*, but to *belong*. Their desperation drives them often to absurd devices, and sometimes humiliating, extreme gestures, in order to make that possible. There is a whole host of social factors making for this desperation: the break-up of traditional communities, the tendency for every industrial business undertaking to become larger and therefore more impersonal, the mobility of modern life, the generation gap. There is a great hunger for contact, belongingness, a need to overcome feelings of alienation and strangeness – especially as the world itself is getting a colder and more threatening place under the shadow of nuclear weapons. Correspondingly, there is a great opportunity for the church to provide for the right sort of belongingness. It hasn't anything to do with getting people to join organizations; it has more to do with inviting people to come and feel warmly accepted in a small group of people who welcome their experience of life, however different, who are helped to believe that they have a contribution to make as well as a gift of friendship to receive. What the group *does* together is less important than what it *is*. If we're church members, we need to ask ourselves a penetrating question: supposing we didn't belong, but felt isolated and lonely, would the church attract us by its quality? Would we feel that we had come home, that this is where we truly belonged?

So we come to the most sensitive and painful area of all: the feeling that we have about ourselves our worth as human beings. These are what Maslow calls our *'esteem needs'*, our desire for

self-respect, self-esteem and the esteem of others, the necessity
to feel that we *count*. This was well illustrated for me by a lady
who was being visited in hospital by another member of the
church congregation. 'Shall I tell the vicar you're in hospital?',
she asked. 'Yes,' said the patient – and then quickly changed her
mind. 'No,' she said, 'let's see if he misses me . . .' Experience
has taught me that if all the people who are troubled or in
despair could be assured that they have value as human beings,
whatever their guilts, fears, unloveliness and feelings of uselessness, then they would be some way along the road to recovery.
The trouble is that they often measure their own feelings of
misery against the image of the successful portrayed in the
media, the ideals held up to them by parents or conventional
church teaching, or sometimes against the *outward* appearance
of their acquaintances – and sink into further gloom. I have
known several first-year university undergraduates who mis-
takenly think that all the others are coping well academically
and living flourishing social lives, when really most of them are
isolated and alienated. Comparisons are always odious, but
never more so than when we compare what we are and aren't
with other people. Then we're denying that uniqueness which is
ours through God's gift. Not to like oneself, not to love oneself,
not to accept oneself, degenerates into hating oneself; and that
is to enter into a pathological condition, whence all sorts of
other ills flow. It is to arrive at the opposite of the truth on which
Christian faith insists: that we are loved creatures of God, whoever or whatever we are. That truth, unfortunately, doesn't
remain uppermost in people's perceptions. Often stretching
back into childhood, there remains the image of an angry God
who spies on you and decrees that some sins can never be forgiven. (How many people have been anxious about that verse
about sinning against the Holy Spirit, and imagined that their
current temptation must be it?) God then becomes for the
adult the God who rejects you rather than the God who
accepts you, and other people's attitude towards you often
seems to reinforce that conclusion. We all have things about us

and in us which are unlovable; but the essential truth is that we are loved not for what we are or aren't, but just because we're *there*, made in God's image. Sometimes going to church seems to make such people's difficulties hard to bear: the image of niceness, pleasantness, don't-we-have-fun-in-Christ's-family can make the person feel more isolated and different still. Exhortations they may hear there to be more loving, more faithful, increase their guilt or widen the gap between where they are and where they think other people are. Only genuine pastoral care can bridge that gap. The truth that we are loved 'where we are right now', what I've called the essential Christian truth, has to be incarnated in the flesh and blood and spirit of one person or a small group of people who are prepared to take the time and trouble to understand what the other person is going through. Simply to listen fully and properly to another person's story *sounds* easy, but really to listen is a rare achievement, and it conveys to that person something of great value. Exercises have sometimes been used, in the practice of group dynamics, in which time has been spent by members of the group just looking at each other, finding something 'nice' to say about each other, genuinely appreciating each other – on the assumption that 'there's a beautiful person struggling to get out'. (God's image?) If we could translate that self-conscious exercise into our everyday dealings with other people, we should begin, quite un-selfconsciously, to heal some of their wounds.

This knowledge of our self-worth assumes greater significance still because of the world in which we live. It has been generally true, since the Industrial Revolution, that society has increasingly seen men and women as functionaries, economic units, there to keep 'the wheels of industry turning'. So a person becomes important, not intrinsically, not in himself, but in so far as he makes a practical contribution to a world of production. That is a deeply-ingrained assumption, which has religious roots in a Calvinistic ethic of the importance of work, and which found some earlier justification in Paul's 'if a man doesn't work, neither shall he eat'.[2] The modern version is the vilification of shirkers and scroungers. (This is not to deny that there are some, but simply to point to the way in which we use the economic yardstick to estimate worth.) Perhaps we can see how false and damaging this hidden assumption is when we consider those who are handicapped. Practically speaking, the handicapped person may not make any *practical* contribution to the prosperity of the country; indeed he will probably have to take from the resources of the welfare state in order to survive: but it would be difficult to find anyone who didn't believe that handicapped people are valuable, just because they *are*. Numbers of parents of handicapped children testify that, despite all their disabilities, the children have given them much more than they as parents have given them. *Clouds got in my way*, by Christine Smith,[3] is the remarkable story of how Christine's parents have only spent one night away from her, although now in her thirties she has a totally helpless and rather grotesque body, due to muscular dystrophy, and many people just can't bear to look at her. It is quite clear that through all their years of sacrifice, the parents feel themselves to be the gainers, not the losers.

Judging a man's worth by his functioning is responsible for much hidden misery in the world. It often lies behind the trauma associated with unemployment, redundancy and retirement, and makes the pains of sick people hard to bear. And aren't the forecasts for the future – little chance of full employment for large sections of the population, shorter working hours, greater leisure, and so on – all pointing to the necessity to expose this assumption? Christian truth about the worth of every individual, irrespective of his gifts or lack of them, his proper functioning or not, was never more topical or relevant than it is today. It wouldn't be too much to claim that in it lies the only hope for a healthy society of the future.

When those four basic needs – physiological, security, belonging and esteem – are satisfied, one may well wonder what others there could possibly be! Their satisfaction constitutes the acme of average expectations. Perhaps our temptation is to get stuck in the gratification of lower needs in the hierarchy, especially in days and areas of deprivation, in the same way in which it is the church's temptation to get stuck in the business of organization and administration. In both cases we are surrendering to a diminished view of life, settling for what has so often been castigated by Christians, though the phrase needs qualification, as a 'materialistic way of life'. ('A pleasant semi-detached, in a nice area, money for holidays and Christmas, a few good friends, and well thought-of – what more is there to life? What else should I worry about?') The mounting incidence of mental illness, the latent frustration and restlessness of so many people, point to the truth that we all have a need within us to be what we must be. Maslow insists that what a man *can be*, he *must* be. That is, must be true to his own nature. Following another psychologist, Goldstein, he calls this process of self-fulfilment 'self-actualization'; and he instances how in one individual it may take the form of being a good mother, in another an athlete, in another an artist, and so on. And when Maslow looked at those deemed to be psychologically healthy, old and young, together with certain characters from history, he discovered that these 'self-actualizers' displayed certain characteristics in common. For instance, they are prepared to accept themselves and others without feeling guilty or defensive: there is about them a naturalness, a simplicity, a spontaneity, an absence of artificiality and a refusal to be bound by convention. They usually have a 'mission in life', some problem outside themselves which takes up much of their energies. They will actually like being on their own, but they will also have especially deep relationships with a few individuals. They will be independent of other people's good opinions or even their affection, and won't be slaves of their environment. They will have an appreciation of the ordinary things of life. When they see a baby for the thousandth time, it will be just as wonderful as if they were seeing it for the first. They will be able to lose themselves in some enjoyment of music or art, some aesthetic, mystical or sexual experience. They will be able to relate to people of different race and colour, will have a sense of humour, and never confuse ends with means. It isn't that such people are perfect or free from faults. They aren't invulnerable supermen; they're subject to the same fears and anxieties as others. But these will arise from looking at real problems outside themselves as objectively as possible, not from a neurotic imagination. They won't, that is, dwell on the negative.

Now this is some portrait of the sort of person all our caring is designed to liberate, and the liberation of the 'psychologically healthy' doesn't differ much from the freedom the Christian knows. 'Psychologically healthy' doesn't mean 'well-adjusted' in the sense of the phrase is usually meant to convey: easy, amiable, predictable, never standing out in any way. Those adjectives could hardly be said to apply to the Jesus who didn't always make things easy for others because he consistently spoke the truth, and whose insights into other people's characters scarcely made him amiable on occasions. His spontaneous reaction to others' needs as he saw them robbed him of being predictable; he could be described as eccentric, and his eccentricity led him to his cross. Such was his 'self-actualization', and it was the opposite of the cool, 'well-adjusted' man. There are other grounds for 'being awkward' than psychological disturbance: it may rather be a sign of health and wholeness. Saints aren't always easy to live with.

Now this says a great deal about the way we are to care, and what our caring should be helping other people to become. They are to be genuinely themselves. In other words, there is no room for trying to make others pale imitations of ourselves. In all our caring we are helping to set free someone, something that is unique in the universe, a creation of God who is to be fulfilled in that potential which God implanted, and which is a person's special and eternal destiny.

There is, then, a response which lay pastoral care can make at every level of human need identified by the psychologists, a response (I would claim) which is potentially made richer and more effective through Christian motivation and insights. But it must be caring for its own sake, and not with the conscious or unconscious aim of making those cared-for Christian. Otherwise, we are subtly slipping over into treating people as means, even if the ends are worthy. The way in which we exercise such unconditional care speaks powerfully for the gospel, and it has often been tragically true that Christians have denied the content of the gospel they are proclaiming through the methods they employ to do so. Christians may rightly feel that every man has a need for the gospel of Jesus Christ, and that this is surely an omission in Maslow's scheme. I would see that gospel operating at every level of human need, rather than at one stratum of it, as is illustrated by our discussion of the response pastoral care makes to human needs. In his discussion of self-actualizing people, Maslow recognizes the force of religious experience, and says significantly that they have the power to love and the ability to be loved. It is surely vastly encouraging that what Christians see in Jesus Christ as the goal of all their striving should be so well characterized in secular terms by secular psychologists as the goal of all human endeavour. That is cause for satisfaction, not mistrust. On the other hand, Christians will rightly feel that their presentation in word and deed of that character, inadequate though it be, their keeping close to him through sacrament and prayer, is a resource which is indispensable to them. It is, of course, also their inspiration to pastoral care. Jesus will be the inspiration of their caring, and their model; and even when his name is never invoked, his will be the presence mediated, seen or unseen.

Finally, lest it be thought that we have been taking Maslow's model too literally, it needs to be said that it is imprecise, and that no one would suggest, and least of all Maslow himself, that his scheme is that into which we all fit, that we must *all* have *all* our lower needs satisfied before we proceed to the next stage. The truth is that we are partly satisfied in our basic needs, and partly unsatisfied at one and the same time. Nevertheless, it is still, I believe, very helpful as a dynamic, but inevitably rough, model of the needs pastoral care seeks to answer, and as some measure of checking our effectiveness. In our consumer society, there is a deal of confusion between needs and wants. High-pressure advertising and salesmanship convince us that we badly need something which countless generations have managed very well without, and our wants become our needs. Our greed is disguised as our need. It is all the more necessary, therefore, to have as clear a view as possible of basic human needs, and the most effective way of answering them.

3

What is Pastoral Care?

What is pastoral care? Two Americans, with the unlikely names of Clebsch and Jaekle, compiled in the mid-sixties a book containing excerpts from pastoral writings from different centuries and called it *Pastoral Care in Historical Perspective*. In their introduction, they define pastoral care as 'helping acts, done by representative Christian persons, directed towards the healing, sustaining, guiding and reconciling of troubled persons whose troubles arise in the context of ultimate meanings and concerns'.[1] That is fairly comprehensive, and when broken down, is extremely useful. In this chapter, I want to explore in detail the four functions of pastoral care they enumerate, but the last phrase 'troubled persons whose troubles arise in the context of ultimate meanings and concerns' also needs examination.

If every single and simple act of goodness or kindness, when pressed to its limits, poses ultimate questions of meaning and value, even more do human troubles point to such questions. The nineteenth-century philosopher, Nietzsche, used to say, 'He who has a *why* to live for can bear almost any *how*', and a psychotherapist, Viktor Frankl, bore this out in his own bitter experience earlier this century. He spent the years of the Second World War in the concentration camps of Auschwitz and Dachau, and when finally he was freed, he learnt that his family had been almost entirely wiped out. But he came to the conclusion that man can bear almost any suffering provided, and only provided, that he discerns some sense of meaning in it. Hence Frankl coined the term 'logotherapy', a process of healing through taking seriously man's search for meaning and purpose. Pastoral care calls out questions of meaning, because as Clebsch and Jaekle indicate, 'it is exercised at a depth where the meaning of life and faith is involved on the part of the helper as well as on the part of the one helped'.[2] Pastoral care, that is, will be exercised by a Christian in accordance with what he believes about the nature and destiny of man, and as we have already seen, the motivation for pastoral care in the first place derives from what he believes not only about man, but also about the eternal nature of God. That will not mean that he will inflict that meaning on others, even if he will always be ready to 'give a reason for the hope that is in him'.[3] It will mean that he will never give up the search for greater clarity, greater depth of understanding of persons and their relationships with each other and with God. He will, that is, always be a student in a life-long educational process.

So to *healing, sustaining, guiding* and *reconciling*.

To be a *healer* (in this sense) is to recognize and understand something of the source of another person's wounds. It isn't to be in the analysis-business, or to pretend to a professionalism which is superfluous. It isn't, either, so to concentrate on the wound that the wound becomes the person and its healer sees a problem and not a person. It is to give the wound space, time, air; it isn't to be ready to apply a miracle cure, or a magical adhesive plaster, or to take away the risk of scars. It is to allow the poison to seep out, and in so doing to be ready to absorb it. If bitterness has been allowed to drain away, scars can be valuable evidence of suffering experienced and transformed. Some wounds are of such long-standing, have cut so deep, that the poison has already done its lasting work; the job of the healer then becomes the job of the guider. Sometimes the wounds are hard to get at, because to avoid the hurt they cause us, we have pushed them hard away, thought they were too painful even to examine; we've found the memory too keen, or the guilt too hard to bear. But trying to forget, trying to act as though they never were, only makes wounds more poisonous still. And the task of the healer we're called to be is gently to help the other to recognize the hidden sore.

There is no trick by which this can be done. It may be that sometimes, and where appropriate, we can help the other person to put his wounds in the context of Christ's wounds, linking our little pains with the great suffering of God in Christ. That will not take the pain away; but it will make it more bearable. Chiefly, and not surprisingly, it will be our own *selves*, our presence, which will be the healing resource, and the more open our presence is to God, the greater our intimacy with him, the greater the confidence, the greater the chance of liberation we shall encourage.

Perhaps, then, to be an *agent* of healing is a more apt phrase to use than 'healer', since it points to the origin and fount of all healing. And to be an agent of healing is also to be an agent of wholeness and salvation, two words or states often spoken of, but not so often thought of as indicating the same condition. Yet the New Testament knows no distinction between them. In the story of the Cleansing of the Ten Lepers, after Jesus had told the leper who has said 'thank-you' to get up and go on his way, the New English Bible reports Jesus as saying, 'Your faith has *cured* you',[4] which is the weakest translation and conveys least what the whole gospel intends; the Revised Standard Version has 'your faith has made you well', which is better; the Jerusalem Bible has 'your faith has saved you', which is better still – but the Authorized Version has 'thy faith hath made thee whole', which is best of all. The word *cure* merely suggests to us getting better from some physical ailment, restoring some part of our body to its proper functioning. But being made well, being saved, being healed or made whole: there's an added and positive dimension. And to be *saved*, to be *healed*, to be *made whole* are all expressed in the Greek New Testament by the same word. Here there is something fundamental. Jesus had sent those ten lepers to the priest to get his certificate of cleanliness; in other words, to act as though they were already healed. And as they went, very obediently – and after all, it was a great act

of faith on their part – their leprosy left them. The men were
made clean, cured. But the implication of the story is that one
man was made whole, which was much more significant. And
why? Because he had been able to express an insight, a percep-
tion, an awareness of gratitude, wonder and humility, to which
the others were blind, and which is an essential part of being
whole. 'Were there not ten *cleansed*?' But 'thy faith hath made
thee whole'.

So we are whole beings. The word 'psychosomatic', which
speaks of the interrelation between mind and body and spirit,
has passed into our common vocabulary, and I know well how
the state of my liver affects my mood and my charity or lack of
it. But our common vocabulary often denies this truth about the
organic unity of a person, the delicate interweaving of the
whole. We talk about Mr Smith's *body* being laid to rest; the
hymn I used to sing as a choirboy was 'On the Resurrection
morning, soul and body meet again'; the Compline prayer we
read at theological college prayed that, 'when our bodies lie in
the dust, our souls may live with thee'. The 1662 Prayer of
Oblation gets it right: we pray that we 'may offer unto thee
O Lord "the wholeness" of *ourselves*, our souls and bodies'. The
National Health Service seems to be beginning to put into
practice what is called 'whole person medicine'. There has been
increasing recognition in the past few years of the interaction
between social, mental, physical and personality factors in the
treatment of individuals, even if there is still a long way to go.
It isn't only our vocabulary which is at fault; it's also our
assumptions. 'When you've got your health you've got everything': if by that we mean that when there's nothing obviously
wrong with you physically, then there's little else to be concerned about, then clearly it won't do. Because, as the grateful
leper implied, there are aspects of human life – insights and
perceptions – to which we all need to come alive if we are ever
to achieve wholeness.

It would be disastrous if we ever believed that we had
achieved wholeness; what is important is that we are on the

way towards it. If we ever thought we'd arrived, then com-
placency would set in and deny our wholeness. There are some
people many of us know who, saving some great leap in medical
knowledge, are unlikely to be cured, made physically better.
But we all know some such people of whom we could never say
that they were not in some way being made whole. Why?
Because, despite their physical infirmity, there is an integration
about them which has used their physical infirmity to good
effect. I remember the girl from Bolton who came back from
Lourdes saying, 'I know now that it's not a matter of going to
Lourdes and being cured. It's a matter of looking to the Cross,
and accepting thankfully that you may not be cured.' There's
the road to wholeness – without physical cure at that moment,
or perhaps ever.

We are whole beings, organic unities; wholeness is that towards which we need to tend. We recognize it instinctively. A
distressed person will often say graphically, 'I'm all shot to
pieces', or more expressively still, 'I've fallen apart'. We need a
magnetic centre which will draw together and unify that which
otherwise would get separated and disjointed. For Christians,
that magnetic centre is God himself: he refers to himself in the
Old Testament as 'I am that I am', the one being who is wholly
integrated. So the measure of the response we make to the
magnetic centre of God and his love is the measure of our
wholeness. And that, paradoxically, means that our capacity
for suffering is also increased. Increasing wholeness can involve
us in increasing suffering. There are many Christian and church
pressures on all of us to be *wooden* rather than imaginative, but
the more imaginatively we respond to God's love in Christ and
to other people, the more sensitive we become, and the greater
the probability that we shall suffer. Any increase in our sensi-
tiveness to what is lovely in the world – and to love – also
increases our capacity for being hurt. That is the dilemma in
which life has placed us: it is the paradox of wholeness. My own
experience is that the more I am involved in other people's
troubles, the weaker, and sometimes the more hurt, I get. It

took me some time to realize that that was almost predictable, and that the alternative was to vegetate on the cabbage-patch!

Being saved, being made whole: sincere Christian people often interpret the gift of salvation far too narrowly. Being saved and being made whole relate to all that it means to be a human being, growing into, and increasingly expressing, that love embodied and disclosed in Jesus. And again, the resultant picture will not be very different from that of Maslow's. It's as exciting as that.

To be a sustainer. Perhaps sustaining, passive and routine-like as it sounds, is that in which we are most engaged; perhaps its worth and its difficulty are much under-valued. To sustain another person is to stay with someone whose illness or grief or anxiety is apparently permanent, so that they may be helped to bear their particular burden, and in the bearing, achieve a measure of personal growth. It is not to tranquilize, or eventually to block off the pain; it is to help put the pain in a larger perspective, and draw its obsessional sting. It isn't to minimize the pain, or pretend it doesn't exist, or subdue it in a welter of cheery clichés. The remark I heard from a well-meaning volunteer in a terminal-care home – 'you'll be better when the weather improves' – is a horrifying example. It is not to allow the sufferer to bear the suffering alone, feel unsupported. It is the ministry of *presence*, of all that being available means. But being present doesn't always mean physically being present. There are times when it is vital to be present: there are times when it is necessary to be *absent*. Jesus' words to his apostles, 'It is expedient for you that I go away', have a wider relevance. There is an art of leaving, *in faith*, an art of creative withdrawal. And growth depends on withdrawal, absence equally with presence.

Sustaining occurs at different levels and at different times of crisis. There is, of course, 'emergency sustaining': the picture that comes to my mind is that of other mourners at a graveside restraining the chief mourner from dramatically throwing himself or herself into the grave at the lowering of the coffin. I like the other picture drawn by D. W. Winnicott in his address to the Association of Caseworkers:

> You are not frightened, nor do you become overcome when your client goes mad, disintegrates, runs out in the street in a nightdress, attempts suicide and perhaps succeeds. If murder threatens, you call in the police to help not only yourself but also the client. In all these emergencies you recognize the client's call for help, or a cry of despair because of loss of hope of help.[5]

Sustaining can mean just accident prevention, or first aid. Then there are occasions when sustaining means being there, when 'there' seems to be a complete impasse and any way forward seems to be blocked. But because one is *there*, ready to listen, ready not to offer any emotional pain-killer or admit defeat, the crisis will lessen and lift. It often happens (and this is what keeps pastoral carers humble!) that things appear to melt of their own accord, and without your having done anything. It only *seems* so: sustaining has been a crucial resource all the way through. Sometimes, sustaining does just mean physical presence – going to court with a mother whose child has been summoned, going to hospital with an older person when he or she is facing a critical medical examination. But mostly, as the word suggests, sustaining is also sustaining over a period of time, being at another's side as he or she works through some personal crisis. One illustration from bereavement may suffice. The most critical time in the process of grief is not immediately on the death of the relative. Then very often, in any case, the bereaved is in a state of shock or numbness and is aided by tranquillizers, as people and messages and letters and flowers pour in. Bereaved people often find themselves at the centre of attention in a way which they may never have experienced in their lives before. But it isn't at that point that they need most support. It is at the point where the numbness and shock are wearing off, and something of the loneliness, the desolation is beginning to dawn, perhaps three or four weeks later. Then is the crucial time; then sustaining matters most. It matters particularly because very often those who are bereaved experience the very opposite of being sustained: I mean, desertion, avoidance by neighbours and friends. Why are we so embarrassed when we don't know what to say? As if words were ever all-important! To have one person who doesn't leave you when you want to express feelings which will be uncomfortable for him and you; who is prepared to go to the bottom of the valley with you, even though they get threatened and muddied in the process: that is the sustaining offered by a true pastoral care.

To be a guider. Here perhaps we are in a danger area. Few things do more to serve our confused motivations of power and doing good than the opportunity to guide someone 'in the right direction'. And if we're committed Christians, and the one to be guided isn't, we may feel we have divine authority for pointing out and putting him on to the right path. Any guidance which assumes its own infallibility, and takes away the freedom of the other person to follow his own path, even if we may think it is mistaken, is wrong and treats the person guided as less than a full human being. Consciously to set out to guide another human being is unconsciously to mould that person in one's own self-image – and what arrogance that is! It is also a denial of the richness, the immense diversity of human beings God's creation gives us. The Tao emphasis on 'letting-be' (or 'non-action') is healthy and wise: 'He who imposes himself has the small, manifest might: he who does not impose himself has the great, secret might. He who "does nothing" effects.'6 Non-action might seem to appeal to our natural indolence: but the more passionately we share convictions, the more difficult such resistance to action becomes. Yet such unconscious moulding of another person is self-defeating in the end, however superficially successful it may at first seem. Consciously trying to exert influence for good inevitably breeds resistance to that influence, as the parent of any child and adolescent learns from painful experience. But we still have influence. Children learn from what they observe in us when we're off guard, saying or doing something we'd rather they didn't learn. (Why does it seem easier to exert influence for evil than for good?) The influence we have for good is that which also happens when we've renounced all eagerness to have such influence. It is an influence of which we're unconscious, and which happens when we're being ourselves, spontaneous, when we've 'let go', and are 'letting-be'. To be grounded in faith enables us to relax and not to try to win a victory – even a victory for God! He will work through our 'being', perhaps even more than our 'doing'.

Of course, there are occasions, and these are at the heart of pastoral care, when disturbed, anxious, troubled friends and acquaintances need our support – and they will often call this guidance, or even advice. Perhaps the only advice which it is right for one person to give another is factual information, or help to disentangle the various elements in a problem. We overstep the mark if, certain urgent crises excepted, we advise another as to 'what to do', not only as Bernard Shaw whimsically remarked, because no human being is good enough to advise another, but because to take away the decision-making process from another person is to preclude growth. Growth occurs when we make choices – and commit ourselves to them, even at cost to ourselves. The limits of guidance, therefore, are set by our willingness to look at several courses of action open to another person, their merits and disadvantages, and then leave the other person to choose. And then we need to support him in and through the choice, even when we might think another course of action would have been more beneficial. A good example of standing by someone who has made a choice which we may regret is that of seeing a girl through an abortion, whatever the pain it causes us. Here we can learn a lot from the wisdom of the experience of those who counsel, and from the well-known accepted secular style of 'non-directive counselling'. Perhaps the irony is that we are guiding best when we're not talking at all, but when we're listening. I can't pretend to be good at it; I only know that it is the most valuable gift we can offer. Yet we're *saying* a very great deal to that person and about that person when we give the whole of our senses and the whole of our selves, as far as is humanly possible, to another in the listening process. We're saying, in the best way possible, that what you have to say to me about *your* human story – which is unique, lived out in God-given circumstances – and therefore about *you*, is so important that I don't want to miss a single fact, echo or nuance. How better can we convey the worth of another human being? Only such effective listening creates confidence in someone else sufficient for them to be able to tell the whole of their story, uncovering all the dark spots, allowing a proper unburdening. Dietrich Bonhoeffer, the German martyr, put it like this:

> Many people are looking for an ear that will listen. They do not find it among Christians, because these Christians are talking where they should be listening. But he who can no longer listen to his brother will soon be no longer listening to God either; he will be doing nothing but prattle in the presence of God too. This is the beginning of the death of the spiritual life, and in the end there is nothing left but spiritual chatter and clerical condescension arrayed in pious words.[7]

The good listener is the one who listens not only with his ears, but with his eyes, with his heart; the one who listens for what is not said, listens to the spaces between the words. And it is an exhausting business.

We never simply listen to *words*: we are discovering the feelings behind the words, and sometimes the feelings we discern and the words we hear may not seem to go together. What we're doing is making it easy for the other person to be himself, and openly express what it is that he feels about the situation in which he's involved at the deepest level. That doesn't mean necessarily that we should encourage the other person to act out in dramatic fashion all that he is feeling in the manner of what is called the 'let-it-all-hang-out' school. We have to recognize angry feelings without those feelings necessarily being forcibly expressed.

Ironically it is that listening which will give the other person the ability to see more clearly what it is that he is saying and meaning. Telling your story to a good listener often helps you to see that story in a new light, and perhaps on occasions such a new light that you see what needs to be done without any active intervention from the listener. (A common counselling experience is to be thanked at the end of an hour for giving your advice, when perhaps not more than a dozen sentences have crossed your lips!)

Of course, there are some who aren't helped except in a negative way by being listened to – or perhaps, they're not really searching for help. They simply want affirmation of their intentions, prejudices and bitterness. (Like the man I passed in the street today who took one look at me, and sounded off at me about the disgraceful state of the road, due to the iniquities of Socialism and Communism!) And we must be sensitive as to when people don't want to talk, and refuse to apply any pressure. There is 'a right time' here as elsewhere, and important though it is, listening is not the only form of caring. What matters is the entering into the other person's world, seeing things with their background and set of values rather than our own, or a preconceived Christian set of values, understanding from within, as if it were our world, without losing our own identity.

There is guidance of another sort: *moral* guidance. Pastoral care may involve us in working out with other people what it is right for a Christian to think and do in a given set of circumstances. Our greatest danger here is to be simplistic, to believe that the issue is perhaps less complex than it is, or to believe that simple reference to gospel texts or phrases like the 'sanctity of life' should or will settle the matter. It may for some, but those same Christians should recognize the hard wrestling, the heart-rending and perplexing dilemmas in which others find

themselves when they try to balance moral factors and come
to what is, inevitably, a grey solution rather than one which is
black and white.

Just over forty years ago, I learnt something I've never
forgotten. The war had started, and my sixth-form friend and I
had to decide whether, as keen young Christians, we should be
conscientious objectors or join up. Naturally, we thought the
Bible would help us make up our minds. So we both went away
and did our scripture homework. And then came back even
more puzzled as to what we should do. For both of us had lists
with – on the one hand, but on the other . . . On the one hand,
Jesus said, 'Resist not evil, turn the other cheek' – but then on
the other, he drove the money-changers out of the Temple with
a whip, and St Paul said we must submit to supreme authorities,
because they are instituted by God. Obviously, we weren't
going to be able to solve the matter simply by appealing to the
Bible. And in the end, one of us decided that war was worse
than the possibility of living under the Nazis, and the other
decided that war wasn't the worst of evils. So one of us joined
the Friend's Ambulance Unit for the rest of the war, and one
of us joined the Air Force as a navigator. And today we're both
ordained ministers, still good friends, living and working not far
from each other. But I've never forgotten that you can't solve
moral questions by turning up black and white answers at the
back of the good book. On every sensitive moral issue today –
abortion and euthanasia are perhaps two obvious examples –
there is always 'on the one hand – but on the other . . .' As one
of my teachers used to say, banging his fist on the table, 'May
no student of mine ever be found saying, "The Bible says," as if
that fixed the matter once and for all. There are always more
questions to be asked . . .' The Bible gives us direction, which
is invaluable. We must not expect it to give us directions.

Take, for instance, the question of the right-to-life of a mongol
baby. The phrase 'the sanctity of life' cannot simply be invoked
to settle the issue. The real, many-sided problems with which
doctors have to deal are problems of immense complexity, but

need practical solutions; the boundary-line is so thin and the possible misinterpretations are so numerous, depending on what standpoint you take. In the end, you may have a solution which strict logic could easily demolish, and earnest moral crusaders shout against – but it may be the course which is the least bad – and in many moral issues, that is the most for which one can strive.

Perhaps the honour lies in the striving and the refusal to dismiss the case with a neat solution. It lies in the serious attempt to come to a mind about it which does justice to the directive of love in which all moral guidance should go, together with all the circumstances of that particular case – and then to live with the consequences of a decision which can never be clear-cut. It is such integrity, such hard-won wisdom that enables growth to maturity to take place. Of course, much of the moral guidance in which we are involved is on a less tense and dramatic scale – the disciplining of someone's adolescent boy or girl, whether a couple should live together, what to do about local vandalism, and so on. But again, taking fully and seriously the situation and circumstances of the case, as well as, for instance, the church's tradition on the particular moral issue and any gospel precepts, is equally important.

To be a reconciler is not necessarily to be looking for the role of dramatic intermediary, or even that of the soft-footed go-between. Of course, there may be times when we are called *to be reconcilers* in a practical way. We may have to receive the confidences of two people whose relationship has broken down; we may have to represent coolly and dispassionately to a third party someone else's grievances. We will then recognize that reconciliation isn't the business of modifying convictions, or asking anyone else to do so; it isn't a matter of speaking other than the truth to accommodate people, or make circumstances easier. (We may sometimes have to speak less than the *whole* truth at any one time.) It's a matter of centring on that essential humanity or, in Christian terms, that oneness in Christ which lies beyond our essential disagreements, and which allows us to be in fellowship with those from whom we differ. Often the disagreements will proceed from something less than conviction, but have been erected into a conviction, and the clear-sighted reconciler will be ready to say so.

The work of reconciliation, then, is chiefly a matter of attitude and bearing: a way of looking at life and other people which is hopeful, and which sees that human solidarity which has always been intuitively perceived by Judaism and Christian faith. It is also to take seriously the cost of forgiveness. Forgiveness must always be free, an act of grace; it can't be deserved or made conditional. But that isn't to say that it's easy. To forgive is to let go of ourselves, the control and direction over our lives. Forgiveness tears us apart, since it involves surrendering ourselves into the hands of the person who has injured us. Forgiveness takes it out of us, burns us up. It is free – but only because the price is paid by the person who forgives. Just as to experience love may humble us into a loving response, so the experience of being forgiven can lead to a response of concern for the one who has been injured, not an attempt to pay the price of forgiveness, which is impossible. The process of reconciliation then becomes the costly business of taking an initiative to forgive, for only that will burst open the locked situation in which two people are held. I am not underestimating the extreme difficulty, and to some, near-impossibility, of loving someone who has injured you and perhaps continues to do so. When the sense of betrayal starts to eat into a person, it can poison the springs of love. But there are examples which can inspire us. One such is the writer Laurens van der Post, who was held during the war in a Japanese prison camp in Java. There he was forced to witness some of the harshest cruelties that man could inflict on man. But it was out of their otherwise bitter experience that he came to see that,

the only hope for the future lay in an all-embracing attitude of forgiveness of the people who had been our enemies.

Forgiveness, my prison experience had taught me, was not
mere religious sentimentality; it was as fundamental a law of
the human spirit as the law of gravity. If one broke the law of
gravity one broke one's neck: if one broke this law of forgiveness one inflicted a mortal wound on one's spirit and became
once again a member of the chain-gang of mere cause and
effect from which life has laboured so long and painfully to
escape.[8]

The initiative, the undeserved act of grace is essential, and as
reconcilers, we can't take initiatives for other people, or urge
such initiatives on them. What we can do is know personally the
cost of forgiveness, and hence the cost of being forgiven, a cost
Christ in some sense took upon himself on the cross. Van der
Post says that he had realized that 'we could take nobody and
no people further than we had taken ourselves'.[9] If that is true
of all pastoral caring, it is especially true of the reconciler.

Chiefly, perhaps, we need to be reconciled to ourselves. The
people who are beset by problems, some of which they recognize as being of their own making, are very often those who
want to run away from themselves, and will frequently say,
'I'll never forgive myself.' That may be the latest step in a long
process of shutting away any parts of ourselves which are not
'nice'. And there has sometimes been a good deal of urging from
Christian faith in that direction. It has often unconsciously
encouraged us to identify only with the light, the good side of
ourselves, and so deny the dark or bad side. But we are all
neither 'good' nor 'bad', but both good *and* bad; and all of us
need to confront our shadowy side and so to integrate and
reconcile. So reconciliation becomes the process of self-
acceptance, which incidentally is one of Maslow's self-actualizing
characteristics and is not the same as being self-satisfied. I am
always struck by the way in which, in contrast to many sickly-
sweet presentations of his character, Jesus was real, and encouraged others to be real. He had the power to make transparent
the characters of those he met, like Mary Magdalene, Zacchaeus

and the woman by the well. And out of that transparency, hope
and a new start emerged. He wasn't afraid, either, of admitting
the frailty in him which made him wince at the possibility of
crucifixion: 'Let this cup pass from me.'[10] Or of feeling desolate
and abandoned and crying out loud, 'My God, my God, why
hast thou forsaken me?'[11] I treasure the fact that as a human
being, he knew what it was like to be me at my worst – when
my 'good image' counts for nothing. And far from being my
despair, I find his injunction to be perfect comforting, since the
word perfect, properly translated, means rounded, complete,
all-of-a-piece, the reconciliation of our dark and light sides.

The more we accept of our lives and character, the more we
have attempted to face fairly and squarely both the 'nice' and
the 'nasty' parts of our nature, the more we shall unconsciously
encourage others to discover freedom for themselves, and come
to terms with themselves.

4

Our Relationships

In Edward Albee's play *The Zoo Story*, the entire action takes place on two park benches on a Sunday afternoon. The two characters, Peter and Jerry, are exchanging confidences about their lives, and Jerry explains how he has unsuccessfully tried to poison his landlady's dog, and what happened the next time he saw the dog:

> I stopped; I looked at him; he looked at me. I think . . . I think we stayed a long time that way . . . still, stone-statue . . . just looking at one another. I looked more into his face than he looked into mine. I mean, I can concentrate longer at looking into a dog's face than a dog can concentrate at looking into mine, or into anybody else's face, for that matter. But during that twenty seconds or two hours that we looked into each other's face, we made contact. Now, here is what I had wanted to happen: I loved the dog now, and I wanted him to love me. I had tried to love, and I had tried to kill, and both had been unsuccessful by themselves. I hoped . . . and I don't really know why I expected the dog to understand anything, much less my motivations . . . I hoped that the dog would understand . . . It's just . . . it's just that . . . it's just that if you can't deal with people, you have to make a start somewhere, *with animals!*[1]

There is an example of a poignant yet common tragedy. To live is to be part of a network of relationships, and to belong and feel at home in such a network is a basic human need. We are born from relationship, however superficial; we are born into relationship, however inadequate our parents; we grow into relationships of various kinds with those outside our family. We need the sustaining which relationships bring if we are going to express ourselves properly as human beings. (Again, 'I need you in order to be myself.') And the question most asked, even about the afterlife is, 'Will I know there those I've known here?' It is obvious, therefore, that relationships of different sorts will form a large part of our pastoral caring, and merit a good deal of examination.

Two dangers we need to recognize from the outset: first, that of trivializing relationships and emptying the mystery of persons and the delicate thread which joins human beings together, by easy hints of the 'you need to get together' sort. 'We have to accept a darker, less fully conscious, less steadily rational image of the dynamics of the human personality,'[2] warns Iris Murdoch. Relationships, subtle and touching the deeps of human nature, cannot without damage be reduced to formulae and easy solutions. Secondly, however, and paradoxically, relationships also can be so exalted, so much talked about, that those who are not part of a happy family with many friends can come to feel that their position is much worse than it really is. We must refuse either to trivialize or over-exalt.

So what do we mean by relationship, and in particular, a healthy relationship? Ugly and unhealthy relationships are evident when we meet someone who is possessed by someone else, or eaten up with jealousy, or manipulated for ulterior motives; worse still, when someone has become somebody's plaything or been made indispensable to another person. Healthy relationships presuppose free beings who have come to know who they are; who have come to a sense, that is, of their own particular and unique identity; and this, it must be said, will have been partly because they have already experienced healthy relationships. So closely interwoven are the faces and fortunes of the human race! When two free beings enter into relationship with each other they are giving themselves to each other, not in order that they may dominate or be dominated by the other person, but simply because it is a good thing to be in relationship. Whatever their abilities in other fields, relationships are the most basic way in which people can be creative. The relationship will be healthy when there is some sort of rhythm of aloneness and togetherness, when there are no feelings either of being suffocated by togetherness or, on the other hand, being deserted and made to feel lonely. It seems to me that those three conditions are crucial: a sense of identity, the ability to give oneself openly, with the recognition of all the hurt as well as the joy that may result, and that rhythm of aloneness and togetherness. I am not, of course, suggesting absolute or impossible ideals. We are dealing with people, and all of us without exception can only approximate, at best, to these conditions of a healthy relationship. But to know those conditions is not only to give us insight and impetus in our own relationships; it is also to help us discern more clearly what is wrong when we meet people who are experiencing great unhappiness, because of a lack of relationships or because of inadequate relationships. We should look at those three conditions separately.

A sense of identity: trouble arises when we are not genuinely free, when we're still tied by emotional bonds or even bonds of gratitude to our parents. The emphasis here is on 'tied'; it isn't that some emotional bonds shouldn't exist. If, however, we are simply looking over our shoulders to see that we are maintaining the moral or personality role that we feel is expected of us, we cannot know ourselves properly. If we are just an extension of someone else, or a replica of something, then we have little of ourselves to give, and true relationship is doomed from the start.

It is when the process of weaning from the child-parent relationship, which ordinarily happens between the age of fifteen and twenty, remains incomplete, perhaps for a long time, that human beings aren't able to detach themselves and offer themselves freely in relationship with another.

Ability to give oneself to another: to give myself is to offer all that I am, weaknesses as well as strengths, in the expectation that I shall be accepted as myself, in my readiness to be hurt, and in my willingness to suffer with the other person. Reciprocally, it means being ready to receive and understand what it is that the other is offering to you. Relationships have been characterized as being of *three* sorts.[3] There are *power* relationships, when two people simply try to take from each other, and an ensuing struggle takes place, with consequent aggressive or defensive behaviour, and one inevitably becomes the loser. One partner feels better because the other feels worse. Then there are *trading* relationships, where there is neither gain nor loss on either person's part, since through compromise tacitly agreed to, both break even. It is, of course, relationship diminished in quality, since any sort of personal bargaining is bound to make a person less than fully himself. There is an absence of conflict, but that is perhaps the most that can be said. Finally, there are *loving* relationships: one person is freely available to the other – at whatever the cost. These three divisions are not important because they help us to place our relationships in categories, and fix them. The truth is that most of the relationships in which we are involved will, to some extent, have something of each in them. It is the clarity which self-knowledge brings us which is important, and the keeping of the third, loving relationship constantly in view. You will notice how a power relationship diminishes the other partner; a trading relationship results in loss and gain on neither side; but a loving relationship enhances the other partner – and that can be mutual.

Rhythm of aloneness and togetherness: relationship is a heightening, not a diminution, of the self, but if this is to be realized, then there must be periods of 'creative withdrawal' from the togetherness or intimacy that relationship entails. Only in solitude can we be fully in touch with those resources which will sustain us in relationship. It isn't only that human nature can't bear too much togetherness; it is that the quality of the relationship becomes more superficial when it is not recreated in separation. Pressure, direct or indirect, from contemporary society indicates to people that to be alone or lonely (and insufficient distinction is made between the two) is something at all costs to be avoided. Accordingly, we seek many escape-routes: not simply alcohol or tranquillizers, but breathless activity, for instance, or some noisy emotional religion, neither of which gives us time or space to face aloneness, and both of which smother the pain of aloneness which is essential to healthy growth. The rhythm of aloneness and togetherness ensures both the preservation of identity and the joy which relationship brings, and deepens its creativity. There is always more of each other to give to each other.

What, then, are the other barriers and hindrances to effective relationships? Chiefly *fear*, shown in the conscious limitations we place on ourselves to avoid the risk of coming too close to another person. It is as if we don't want to come any nearer than is absolutely necessary for the way in which we can feel safe with the part we want the other person to play, the 'limited liability' notion we have of the relationship. There are other fears, especially in struggling to make the first attempts to forge a relationship at all. Often, we fear that we shall make fools of ourselves, or not know how to 'control' ourselves. The bogy of 'control' and 'self-control' lies behind a lot of ineffectual relationships. We feel afraid that we shall make mistakes from which we shall never be able to recover or retrieve ourselves. We may lack proper self-confidence because the high expectations placed on relationship are such common knowledge and we feel we shall never be able to 'perform' in relationships satisfactorily.

The ingredients, then, of healthy relationship are the freedom recognized in oneself which is respected in self-acceptance, and in the acceptance of others, and the readiness to be completely available to the other person, without losing one's identity.

The Christian believes that at the heart of the universe there is the mystery of relationship. Since the 1960s, there has been much loose jargon talked about Christian involvement in relationships. I like the satirical graffiti which came out of St John's University, New York:

> Jesus said to them, 'Who do you say that I am?' They replied, 'You are the eschatological manifestation of the ground of our being, the kerygma of which we find the ultimate meaning in our interpersonal relationships.' And Jesus said, 'What?'

There is something much more direct and profound that is at the heart of Christian faith. The much-maligned doctrine of the Trinity, Father, Son, and Holy Spirit, stands for and symbolizes the distinctiveness of each Person, their equality, and their complementarity. There is another and equally essential truth in the Trinity; that this circle of relationship isn't a closed circle. It isn't only the self-giving of each for and to the other, but also to the life of the world. It is a circle which is always open, and from the magnetic mysterious centre there radiates that stream of outgoing love which draws us into the circle and takes us up into the Godhead. That should say something to us about relationships which are turned in on themselves and their own preoccupations, or absorbed simply in the welfare of those involved in the relationship. Here caution is necessary, for a relationship may still have worth and quality even if it isn't turned outwards. There's obviously something wrong if, for instance, two people are so diverted to activities outside themselves that when they do come together, their interests are so divergent that the form of relationship between them is weakened. Often the pathetic discovery of retirement is that, faced with the prospect of togetherness for the first time for many years, two people discover, not the richness which is between them, but the poverty. But two people in a healthy relationship will be able to make anyone who comes into the circle feel at home, and will see them as someone incorporated within the relationship itself.

It sounds as if I'm suggesting that given the right conditions of relationship, then everything will come right just like that. We know that it will never be like that; it is always less satisfactory and more exciting than that, at one and the same time. The truth is that our needs shift and vary, and because (albeit unconsciously) we find the satisfaction of those needs in other people, our response to those people changes as well. Other people do what we do, take from others what they need when they need it, and therefore some relationships which seem all-important one moment may seem to die a temporary death the next. It isn't a matter of conscious or deliberate deception, or letting down – though it may tragically appear so. We need to recognize that what we judge in others as fickleness or betrayal simply refers to that same fragility which, if we're honest, we're forced to recognize in ourselves. Perhaps the best friendships are those which can happen between two people who don't see a lot of each other, enjoying each other's company when they do; and the ensuing silence doesn't spell indifference, for each knows that at the summons of a telephone call, the other will be there, available, predictable, *the same.*

> Who, when great trials come,
> Nor seeks nor shunnes them; but doth calmly stay,
> Till he the thing and the example weigh;
> All being brought into a summe,
> What place or person calls for, he doth pay.
>
> Whom nothing can procure,
> When the wide world runnes bias from his will
> To writhe his limbs, and share, not mend, the ill.
> This is the mark-man, safe and sure,
> Who still is right, and prayes to be so still.[4]

One harmful assumption which married people can make is that there must be something odd about someone who is single. Loose talk, even when spiced with humour, often makes single people feel failures, or at best, second-class, when they are probably being most courageous and self-actualizing by remaining unmarried. We must not see the single state as one necessarily without relationships. Being single may, and often does, free someone for a great variety of relationships with other men and women in a wide age-range. Indeed, some single people feel more 'related' than many of their friends who are apparently happily married, but locked into a domesticity which can be quite stifling. If the sexual orientation of the single person is largely homosexual rather than heterosexual (and this must never be tacitly assumed of single people), then it is for pastoral carers to recognize their considerable difficulties in achieving a 'stable relationship' and offer appropriate support. It is not for us, whatever our Christian or moral stance on the subject, to set out to alter them – or, worse still, reform them! The implications of the way in which the church orders its worship and life sometimes makes it difficult for the single person, despite the fact that of all the forty-year-old men and women in this country, only half are once-married, with children. In an article in *Theology*, Michael Johnson criticizes the way in which the church makes excessive use of symbolism from married and family life, since it seems to suggest that fulfilment is available only to those who conform to that rigid social pattern.

> While the Church in the first centuries of her life stressed the virtue of celibacy and virginity to the detriment of marriage, the Church in our own time has gone too far the other way in rehabilitating the married state, with the result that no support is available from the average congregation for the single person.[5]

The emphasis many local churches put on Family Communion and family services makes many single and divorced people feel more unwanted than the church often intends. Perhaps every church needs to ask itself: to what extent are we implicitly cold-shouldering or genuinely treating with welcome and with warmth those who are single? How far are we recognizing that the single state has an intrinsic worth?

Glorification of the family in Christian and church life can have other undesirable effects. In our proper insistence on a stable family life as part of God's ordering of creation, and essential to healthy, human society, we need also to remember two other equally important truths. The first is the ambivalence with which Jesus himself seems to have regarded the family. He was prepared to admit that the family had claims on us, but he asserted almost vehemently that those claims were not supreme. 'Who is my mother? Who are my brothers? Whoever does the will of God is my brother, my sister, my mother.'[6] He always seems to have laid an emphasis on obeying God as a first priority, even if it meant, as it did in his own case, leaving one's own family. Some of the harshest words he is reported to have spoken concern our duty, as disciples, to break with our own families. That brings me to the second truth. It is easy to lose sight of the fact that families are means to ends, not ends in themselves. We are placed in families to grow as human beings, and then to outgrow those families. A parent's task is to work himself out of a job, even if he is never, whatever happens, to lose his love and care. We have to recognize the way in which suffocating family life can be destructive of personal growth. As pastoral carers we shall never simply be devoted to the preservation of the family at all costs.

Obviously, if the first one-to-one relationship we normally experience in our lives is that between ourselves and our parents in the family, the second for many people is in marriage. There has been increasing emphasis this century on the relationship-aspect of marriage. This, in turn, led to high expectations of the return marriage offers in terms of personal enrichment, and a greater facility for changing partners when those expectations are disappointed. Whereas social and economic conditions in the past kept the partners (in particular, women) to the importance of contract in marriage, today there is a return to the idea, to be found both in the Old and New Testament, of marriage as the community of relationships of love. The covenant relationship in the Old Testament between God and his chosen people is compared to marriage: St Paul compares the marriage-relationship to that between Christ and his church. This positive view of marriage as *relationship*, in which each partner potentially finds fulfilment in and through the other, is a view which should find an echo in Christian hearts and minds. Very often it appears, on the contrary, as if Christians are simply denouncing a mounting divorce-list and wishing for a return to the days when marriage-expectations were lower. In his many writings on the subject, Jack Dominian has described marriage as being a matter of sustaining, healing and growth – and it's no accident that this description comes so close to that of a description of pastoral care with which we have worked. *Sustaining* is the support, physical and emotional, given in situations 'for better, for worse, for richer, for poorer, in sickness and in health'. *Healing* is the healing of the wounds each brings to the marriage as a result of their experience of life so far. When both partners up to that point have experienced such deprivation, dependency and inadequacy that they have few resources of healing to offer to each other, then difficulty arises at the outset. *Growth* occurs when each partner demonstrates the love they feel by a closeness which is able to reach the inner world of the other and bring a sense of wholeness and completion. It is as if we need the close presence of another person to help our real and best selves to emerge.

When we begin to look at marriage in these terms, we shall be saved from those legalistic and harsh or impersonal judgments which Christians are tempted to rush into 'in defence of the gospel'. We shall take seriously the *quality* of relationship rather than seek simply to assert the necessary permanence of that relationship, come what may. In other words, we shall be doing what a true pastoral care always inspires us to do: keeping close to the deep needs of persons. Monica Furlong writes:

Is it that we would rather sentimentalize marriage than look attentively at the very real pain that many married people suffer? One of the difficulties about the pain of marriage is that for reasons of loyalty there is a convention of silence about marital difficulty except among the closest friends; most of us have been astonished when, at some time or other, we have learned that some couple whom we believed to be living in perfect harmony have been wretchedly miserable for years. Maybe it is that the better a marriage, the *more* a couple can be open in a quite relaxed way about their difficulties; it is only the rockiest marriages that have to keep boosting a public image of rapturous happiness.[7]

Many of us will rightly feel that lay pastoral caring doesn't take us into the delicate and expert areas of marriage-counselling, for which, in any case, special agencies exist. But there are few of us who won't at some time or another be involved in a couple's marital breakdown, and then we shall be called upon to display all the qualities which counsellors are encouraged to develop. We must refuse to be judgmental and take sides. We must not be despairing when what seem to us to be eminently practical solutions don't work. We have to recognize that marriage problems aren't amenable to rationality; we are in the realm of the emotions and of deep-seated hurts. So far as we can, we must see the situation as the other person sees it and according to his value-framework. We shall, that is, be responding to the persons who are encountering problems, rather than simply confronting the problems themselves. It will again be our listening which will not only help the other person to sort out what is going on, but will be our chief means of support. It will in no way be our responsibility to decide the outcome, whether the relationship should be terminated or not, but our listening will help to clarify the situation for those involved. Moreover, we can offer some very practical help: some relaxed meals, a bed, a quiet room, some financial assistance where necessary. What is desperately important is that we should help them not to feel outcasts or unwanted because they're no longer part of the 'happy couples' of which (even today) society only seems to approve. The church, too, often seems particularly efficient at providing a disapproving community. My experience is that people in the midst of marital breakdown feel that they can no longer attend church, not only because it will sharpen their guilt, but also for fear of what the congregation will say – or the way in which some members will just look at them!

Many of the situations in which we're likely to be involved will have at their heart the business of commitment. What makes painful situations worse is the way in which Christians give the impression that we simply need to be committed to commitment. Often, for instance, the church seems to be commending the commitment of marriage simply as a commitment, without any serious regard to the wounds and scars, and what feel like the lasting hurts, of one or both the two partners involved. It is as if we are simply expected to show the stiff upper lip and hold grimly on, since it is the loyalty implicit in the commitment, rather than people's needs, which seems to be of supreme importance. That is one side of the picture: the way in which commitment, simply persisted in, against all the evidence of the quality of relationship, very often diminishes those involved.

> Each of us may give another person love and help in inner growth for a while. But in a changing world, with changing people, why should we expect that love to last for ever or denigrate it if it does not? Why should love, once a mansion, be made into a cage through false expectations of what love is?[8]

The conclusion would seem to be obvious, that where commitment damages the people concerned, the commitment should be terminated. But there is an equal fact of experience to be weighed. Because our commitments are bound up with our identities as persons, and because we are who we are through the commitments we make, there is a sense of the disintegration of the self when commitments are broken – on both sides. The one who suffers the breaking of the commitment feels betrayed, and very often decides, untrue to his own generous nature, that he is not going to lay himself open to the possibility of being betrayed and hurt again. One more personality shrivels up and withers.

If our task as pastoral carers is not to act as marriage-guidance counsellors, still less perhaps is it to act as experts in sexual matters – even though sometimes we may have to listen to some peculiar stories! We need, I think, generally to relax about the subject. That doesn't mean that we don't take seriously the tremendous power the sexual drive asserts over our lives, and all the hurts and misunderstandings, frustrations and divisions it can cause. But it is precisely because of this that I suggest that we should relax. Admittedly, we have to have a strong sense of our own identity and self-worth to do this; but I believe that we must be ready to fly in the face of all the pressure which the conventions of a so-called 'permissive society' place upon us. Today, we are the victims of a sort of sexual tyranny which makes us believe that if we don't have sexual experience in a certain way, there is something wrong with us, or perhaps worse still, wrong with our partner! It's a tyranny which enforces expectations of performance on us, as if we were engaged in some sort of game or sport in which it is vitally important to win. The result is that we devalue moments of tenderness and gentleness which are as important as any correct sexual 'technique'. Perhaps the most important guide-line is to see the way in which the physical expression should be appropriate to the level of the relationship between two people and the commitment implied in it. Inappropriate physical gestures quite rightly repel us: they are an invasion of our person. The arm round the shoulder, or the taking of the arm, can patronize us. To confuse levels of physical expression is to damage relationships, and hence the people involved in the relationships. Morality has a lot to do not just with prohibitions, but with the implicit integrity of the right physical expression of the right emotional level.

The psychologist Carl Gustav Jung used to say that when people brought sexual questions to him, they invariably turned out to be religious questions, and vice-versa. We need to keep

the connection constantly in mind, not negatively but positively. What we believe about the love of God and so about respect for persons made in God's image, tenderness and compassion – all this is reflected in our intimate relationships. Perhaps the truth is that when we really love God, we then become better lovers!

We must finally return to Albee's play , *The Zoo Story*. What about Jerry in the play, the many Jerrys who feel imprisoned, unable to break out of the high walls which circumstances, they and other people have built? No one can make relationships for another, and it is a difficulty most 'helpers' encounter that even when they see so clearly what it is that is causing such pain, unlike the medical profession, they are powerless to provide a remedy. Sometimes to those who find themselves unable to start a relationship, good 'advice' makes things worse by increasing the sense of incompetence or guilt. Often the phrase 'be more outgoing' is used – as if the will weren't paralysed. (Imagine going to a social club when you don't know anybody – to *make* friends, as we say.) Exhortations to 'be more loving', often heard in church, heighten the misery – since that is precisely what their condition seems to preclude. 'You've got to make a start somewhere . . .' All we can seek to do is to be alongside Jerry as he attempts brick by brick to take down the walls of his own prison. It's as slow and as painful as that. And the fact that someone begins to talk about their isolation means that at least the faint beginnings of a new relationship are there – and that is the starting-point for self-acceptance and the acceptance of others.

We can also do a little self-examination. Are we the sort of people who are sufficiently open to, and aware of, others' needs that the more obvious barriers to relationship in *us* are removed? The good opinion we have of ourselves often deceives us. I've always thought of myself as a friendly sort of chap, at home with most people, ready to do anyone a good turn. But recently, I had reported to me how one of my colleagues sees me. 'Standoffish', 'a bit arrogant', 'looks after himself' . . . Of course, he's right. Unfortunately, that *is* the other side of me, and it was good for me to be brought face to face with it. My only comfort was that if that is true of me, then it must also be true of others. So we need to ask ourselves: are we the sort of people to whom others would naturally and normally relate? Are we sufficiently flexible, wide in sympathy and understanding? And how often are we prepared to take those same initiatives in relationships which we expect others to take towards us?

5

Three Ages of Man

Just as every age is an age of transition, so any period can be a
period of crisis in personal life. Nevertheless, there are three
periods which merit especial attention, and which seem to pose
particular problems: adolescence, middle age and old age.
What contribution can pastoral care make towards their
resolution?

Adolescence

Many adolescents undergo extremely acute suffering mentally
and emotionally, in what is a period of bewildering physical
change and considerable personal and social pressures. That
needs to be recognized first, since older people seem to find it
hard to have any compassion towards the noisy, awkward,
rebellious, rude, volatile creatures that adolescents often are.
(We find it difficult to remember that four or five years earlier,
we were seeing them as delightful little boys and girls.) Their
earlier physical maturing fits uneasily with a lack of experience
of life and a world of confused moral values; increasing numbers come from broken homes or single-parent families, and
haven't the experience of a healthy and balanced family-life;
they are an easy target for much of the advertising world since
in many cases (the unemployed excepted) their spending power
on non-essentials is considerable; above all, they have inherited
a world which seems to offer little hope of personal or global
stability in the future, and in which inequalities abound to make
the rich people and countries more prosperous, and the poor

more poverty-stricken. This is the world in which they are to make their mark and develop a life that is worth living. The severe pressures on them to conform to fashion, be it in clothes, music or general life-style, leaves many lonely and isolated; and just at the stage when they have begun to 'see through' their parents, they have no one to whom to turn for solace and encouragement.

It is here, I believe, that as lay pastoral carers we have a great deal to offer to adolescents. Of course, their suffering isn't their only characteristic, but until we can begin to feel their world as they feel it (and that is extremely hard for those of us who are products of a very different age), we cannot be of much help to them. Our natural inclination is to 'advise' them or, worse still, be censorious about their way of life: that widens the generation-gap rather than bridges it, and it's interesting to see how on the whole we older people blame the younger for the existence of that gap at all. Once we begin to get under their skin, we can appreciate many of their gifts and qualities: their honesty (very painful to see at times, for it illuminates our own hypocrisies), their care for justice, and often, their generosity. Few things are more impressive, because confidence in this respect is extremely hard-won, than a relationship between an older person and an adolescent in which the adolescent is able to talk freely, even about intimate matters, without feeling that he is going to be judged and thought less of for so doing. This is rare, but it is possible, and I have seen it happen in the context of normal parish life. I recall the way in which one lady, whom you would have recognized as having all the characteristics of the middle class, got to know well two rough lads from bad homes, and acted as confidante to them in their very different circumstances. True, there was an occasion for meeting: the lady dispersed Coca Cola three times a week in the lads' club, to which the boys belonged. That example points to the importance of local provision by churches for this sort of pastoral care of adolescents. All youth work in our churches has become harder and harder in the last twenty-five years, as young people have become more sophisticated, with more money to spend and the consequent greater freedom of choice. No longer can the churches cater for many of the leisure-time needs of adolescents: it is not only useless to try and compete with other agencies, but in many cases wrong. There are some areas, of course, where the clubs that the church can still provide on a simple basis will be the only facilities which exist for young people, and then the opportunities for friendships such as I have mentioned are possible, when older people who see the importance of pastoral care are prepared to be regularly involved in the running of the club, and where young people are ready to include them. (I don't minimize the difficulties in this: the sacrifice of a night or two every week, the risk of vandals and even of violence.) Clubs are either 'organized friendship' or they aren't worth time and trouble spent on them. But what above all is necessary is that there should be a place where older people and younger people can *really* meet (and the *really* is important), so that out of that meeting over a period of time, and quite spontaneously, friendships can grow and, when it is necessary, adolescents can share their difficulties with at least one other person. One valuable way of doing this is through honest discussion of what we believe, and why; and what difference such beliefs make in our experience of life.

This isn't as tame and trite as it appears. Adolescents have three needs in particular. First, they are searching to discover who they are, trying to reconcile attitudes and ideas they have imbibed from their own family background with those they have come up against in the wider world, and so, of seeing where they stand. Secondly, they are very often feeling great guilt about sexual matters and about their own attitude to people and life in general. And thirdly, they are looking for a framework of values in which to see their lives, and give them landmarks for the future. In all these needs, pastoral carers can help through their unconditional friendship. One of the ways in which the adult friend will help will be in the gentle but piercing asking of questions about attitudes. Adolescents are often totally dogmatic or idealistic in their views. I recall expecting the world to be completely saved by socialism and pacifism when I was eighteen. It is important, however, not to settle for the old adage which simply suggests to young people, as it comes over to them with all the cynicism of age, 'You'll grow out of it!' Questioning is helping them to see that the matter may be more complicated than at first they thought, and so needing further depth of investigation. From an early age, we take our values unconsciously from those whom we come to admire rather than from any attempt on the part of others to teach us directly. So we can relax, let be. Our friendship will be the source of moral values for others – for better or for worse!

In this way, the lay pastoral carer will be unconsciously demonstrating his own commitment to Christian faith and, incidentally, helping the adolescent in this vital matter of commitment. Some religious cults operating mainly in the States, but increasing over here, have caused much distress to parents of adolescents, who have seen their children, as it were, taken into slavery, by the wholesale irrational commitments such cults demand.

Two apparently contradictory features seem to be marks of the moral climate in which we live. One is the seemingly increasing willingness on the part of often intelligent young people to commit themselves to such fanatical sects: the commitment is total to the point of dehumanization. The other feature is the strong temptation to lead lives where any commitment is seen to be cramping and restricting, damaging to any possibility of a fulfilled and enjoyable life. Underlying this is the notion that to own no final loyalties, no binding commitment, is the only sure road to fulfilment. (Here perhaps it should be remembered that to refuse commitment is still in one sense to be committed – to neutrality.) Adolescents in extreme sects are said to come in the main from affluent and fairly privileged homes where it is possible to buy your way out of or into everything. Is the impetus to commitment in such cases something to do with the way in which they recognize the emptiness which marks the life in which all commitments are seen to be infantile, regressive and imprisoning? They perhaps see hollowness for what it is worth. Of course, all this is only to underline the importance of our own commitment, which in its turn radically affects other people. It might even make us ask the question, 'To whom or what are we committed?' at greater depth.

I like the analogy I once came across, comparing the world of the adolescent to a football field. He must have plenty of space to move in, kick the ball about, so to speak, experiment in attack and defence, prove himself; but there must also be a clearly-defined pitch, with well-marked sidelines; there must be not only a first-aid man ready with his sponge, but a referee who will be there in the background, ready to blow his whistle as little as possible. It is the privilege of pastoral carers to be both first-aid man and referee! There perhaps the analogy breaks down a little: the pastoral carer isn't only impartial, he is on the side of the adolescent as well.

Middle age

The recognition that middle age often represents a time of personal crisis is fairly recent. Previously, it was assumed that only the early and latter stages of life needed particular concentration: in the period between, you just muddled through! Now we see much more clearly that the vague feelings of dissatisfaction with life which seem to accumulate especially between the ages of thirty-five and fifty-five bring on problems which are as acute as those of any other age-group, but which have received much less sympathetic attention.

Social factors at present, such as unemployment and redundancy, have immeasurably exacerbated features already at work nurturing tension and unhappiness. For middle age is primarily a slow arriving at a moment of truth. It is the point at which we are able to look both backwards and forwards, and often not to like what we see. Looking back, we see that the qualities and difficulties we recognized in ourselves at an earlier stage in life still persist, and may have hardened; and that we carry around with us problems from long ago which are still unresolved. We are the same as we were – only more so. Worse still, perhaps, we begin to see those same sad qualities reproduced in our children. We see, too, the hopes and ambitions we entertained at an earlier stage in life unfulfilled. As we peer into the future, there may seem little likelihood either that we shall be able to change, or that we shall ever realize those ambitions. We seem so stuck in our frustrations that we can become the easy victims of disillusionment and cynicism. Increasing physical limitations remind us that old age is round the corner. Death has ceased just to be a remote possibility which happens to other people, but begins to assume a real shape for us, and the incidence of road accidents and coronary thromboses increasingly fill it out.

Of course, a lot of our frustration is to do with unrealistic expectations that we have harboured or that have been fostered in us by the social forces of the age, and in particular by mass-media. The false and unreal dogma that we all deserve a higher standard of living year by year is matched maritally, as we have seen, by too high a degree of expectation as to what relationship can offer and achieve; and further, that instant remedies, strikes in one case and divorce in the other, can effect a change for the better. Unspoken-of failure is a constant feature of middle age. In career terms, if you have gone as far as you can go by the age of forty, you tend to reckon yourself as a failure; if, on the other hand, you are a success in the world's terminology, you perhaps despise that success, and see how little inner peace it brings. In both cases, the middle-aged person seems to be the loser.

Once he has come to terms himself with his own middle age, the pastoral carer has, I believe, a lot to offer to those who seem beset with its difficulties and see few, if any, of its opportunities and advantages. The fact that, biologically, we are superfluous after the age of forty, that we have reproduced ourselves in our nuclear families, seems to me extremely symbolic. It is no coincidence that so many women between the ages of thirty-eight and forty either have or want to have one last child; otherwise, they feel, they would face life without a clear role. Increasingly our working lives are shorter and shorter as longevity increases, and this, too, shifts the emphasis from our significance as *useful* human beings to our own intrinsic worth. In other words, middle age can be the point at which we can become sufficiently detached, sufficiently removed from attachment to false values that we can begin to appreciate human life for what it is, now that we understand its proper limitations.

Perhaps our understanding of limitations is the key to middle-age health – and beyond. Our growth as human beings and the growth of civilization seem to depend on rebellion against limits in life. In his massive *Study of History*, Arnold Toynbee concluded from his survey of twenty-seven civilizations that civilization started to flourish when people had the right amount (not too many, not too few) of physical limitations to struggle against, and were able to make the right response to a reasonable challenge. The same is true of much creative work, and certainly of the visual arts. The psycho-analyst Rollo May tells the story of how Duke Ellington explained that since his trumpet player could reach certain notes beautifully, but not other notes, and the same with his trombonist, he had to write his music within those limits. 'It's good to have limits,' he remarked. Rollo May went on to say that Michelangelo's writhing slaves, Van Gogh's twisting cypress trees and Cezanne's yellow-green landscapes of southern France are all great works of art, because whilst they have spontaneity, they also have that mature quality which comes from the absorption of tension, and that, in turn, is the result of the artist's successful struggle with and against limits.[1]

So limits are valuable, and the struggle against them healthy and conducive to our growth. To keep on trying to push back bit by bit the limits in our lives is essential; the saddest people are those who have nothing to fight for and against. But that is only half the story. Futile struggle against certain inescapable limits can only produce frustration and bitterness; acceptance of those limits and working within them, on the other hand, can bring a deal of satisfaction and happiness. We all know some people who, having accepted the inescapable limitation of some physical handicap like deafness, seem to transcend the limitation because of their acceptance of it. One of the most contented people I've known, a cousin of mine, deaf from birth, spends his life helping other deaf people with their problems. Even so, none of us ever fully transcends our limitations, especially those placed upon us by our heredity and early upbringing; we may try to deny them, we may sometimes use them to good advantage, but the effects of them never finally leave us. And when we remember that Jesus was born of poorish parents in a crowded little house in a small, backward, powerless nation right on the circumference of the Roman Empire, we can see clearly that it isn't outward circumstances in our lives which are totally conditioning. What matters more is our self-knowledge and self-acceptance: our self-knowledge which helps us to see and know those limitations which are our particular and real limitations, and that self-acceptance which allows us to accept ourselves, whatever our gifts or lack of them. We sometimes oscillate between two poles: on the one hand, of thinking that it's only other people who have limitations and not us – and on the other, that of thinking that because we're lazy and unimaginative, we have limitations which can never be overcome. Many of the tragedies in world history have been caused by those of the first sort, men and women who have considered themselves sovereign or infallible and almighty; much of the real encouragement in world history has come from those who have triumphed over what at first sight seemed like paralysing limitations.

Now world history may seem some way away from the crises of our own lives in middle age. But middle age is above all the point in our lives when to see limitations clearly for what they are is essential to stability and happiness, then and thereafter.

So we may well need the help of someone else, some pastoral carer, who by his candour and honesty will help us discover in ourselves those limitations which only limit us because we choose to do nothing about them, and those limitations which are ours because that is how God made us, and which we simply have to accept. The role of the pastoral carer, here and often elsewhere, is that of being a personal aid to self-knowledge, one who helps us pray that prayer of Reinhold Niebuhr the theologian with real meaning: 'God grant us the serenity to accept what cannot be changed, the courage to change what can be changed, and the wisdom to know the difference.'

The elderly

We are perhaps made more aware of the needs of the elderly than those of any other section of the community. These needs seem obvious, and we hear of several welfare organizations which cater for them, from Age Concern to Meals-on-Wheels. What is less realized is the constantly increasing number of those over the age of sixty-five which, we're told, will represent just over fifteen per cent of the population by the end of the century; and the way in which the gap between their obvious needs and the ability of the welfare organizations to supply them is also increasing all the time. There will always be room for more voluntary involvement in luncheon clubs, transport schemes and the like, and the Age Concern Action Guide, *What Can We Do?*[2], could be used to stimulate many initiatives by local churches in these and other directions.

There is every reason to be practical. But there is one particular contribution which Christians and Christian faith can make in this area of human concern, and therefore of pastoral care. The International Year of the Disabled was a considerable success in drawing attention to the needs of the disabled and in helping pressure to be put upon local authorities and organizations to make better provision for them. Where it seems to have been less conspicuously successful was in the matter of encouraging people to see the disabled as people like themselves, in changing fundamental attitudes. This was a particular dimension of interest, one would have thought, for the church. (I blush for the church in my own area in this respect. In a series of three one-day schools promoted at Manchester Cathedral, two were on 'Women and Theology' and 'Sacraments, East and West', and both recruited between thirty and sixty students. The third, on 'The Church and the Disabled', in which such modification of attitudes was the main theme, recruited two students only.)

It seems to me that it is in this matter of attitudes that, as pastoral carers, we make our particular contribution to the welfare of the elderly. Even in some of the best-run clubs for older people, the impression sometimes given is that older people are to be treated as children, to be patronized and given sweets, that they may expect to receive all but have little to give. Older people can obviously be awkward and cantankerous: unlovely characteristics displayed earlier in life can become exaggerated in later life. But we do not begin to tap the wisdom and the life older people still have to offer. Given sufficient leisure and patience to listen, many of them have fascinating stories to tell about their earlier lives. Ronald Blythe's book, *The View in Winter*, is just such a collection of fascinating stories of people from very differing backgrounds, and makes us realize how gloomily we are preoccupied with,

> this new fate of an old age for everybody. But we never say, as we might with any other general advancement, 'How wonderful it is that by the year 2000 everybody will be more or less guaranteed of a full life!' Instead we mutter, our faces thickened with anxiety, 'Just think, in twenty years' time half the population will be over sixty.'[3]

Our present cult of youth has made us value far too little the contribution older people can make, given sufficient encouragement, to our common lives. The familiar caricature of an old grandmother sitting in the corner being quiet and not interfering is redolent of an attitude we like to foster, but even that is too hopeful, since today it is more likely that grandmother will be removed from the family, and put in an institution of some kind. Older people feel they have to fight continually for their dignity, their self-respect, their right to be taken seriously; and the paradox is that the better we provide for them in material ways, the greater that fight becomes. Apart from physical infirmity, they have the additional difficulty of seeing their loved ones and friends depart from this life, one by one: for them, bereavement is seemingly a constant process, and increasing loneliness a real threat, which is often unadmitted because of their pride. All this means that self-esteem and self-worth, which is of the essence of humanity at whatever stage in life, needs constantly to be nurtured. At the emotional and spiritual level, older people are, of course, threatened very much by change, and the speed of change in every sphere of their lives is completely different from what it was when they were younger. How often is there anyone who really has the time and patience to talk through with them the effect that the speed of change is having on their inner lives? And when they read and hear of such dramatic changes in Christian thinking as are proposed by the *Myth of God Incarnate*, or are faced with Alternative Service Books, they need very gently to be helped through the changes, instead of being dismissed as those who are incapable of understanding the reasons for the changes.

Regular visitation of older people is an obvious example of the way in which this is done. I stress 'regular' because especially if you're housebound, and look forward to a particular point at which someone comes to see you, then the sense of being let down and disappointed is bitter if it doesn't happen and you're not warned in advance. By definition, those most on their own and who need to be 'discovered', since they are less obvious, are in most need of such visitation, and churches are best-placed in local areas to locate them. Nor must we tolerate the heresy that visiting by anybody but the minister from the church is 'second-class': in my judgment, it is only the laity who are able to do 'first-class' visiting in the sense of giving plenty of time to one or two people, for the minister's time will be occupied in visiting more people for 'official' reasons like communion at home, or seeing the sick in hospital. There are several jobs which older housebound people can do for the church – and I'm not only thinking of making soft toys for the bazaar, even though that's important too! House-groups could sometimes meet (even though in some places there may be practical difficulties) in the homes of older people, to ensure that they are still able to participate. Above all, perhaps, older people, no longer able to be physically active or able to take much part in social activities within the local church, feel privileged to be asked to intercede regularly for one or two people. It isn't necessary that they know much about the circumstances of those for whom they intercede, although clearly the more links that can be made which fill out their imagination, the better. We haven't begun to explore very far yet the latent spirituality in older people who are housebound, and who have the leisure and the space in a way in which others may not have. The development of such spirituality in older people presupposes that some lay pastoral carers will feel that they have the capability and confidence to help here – and that may to some of us seem a lot to ask. We may wish to leave responsibility for this to 'the minister', whose professional task it is. That would be a pity. The strengthening of our own lives of prayer can come from sharing with one another our own insights gained from experience and our own difficulties as much as from formal instruction (if not more so). Courses of formal instruction about prayer rarely seem to help some people who actually need to be strengthened in their own individual approach. We need to become as natural in our approach to prayer as we are, for instance, to Meals-on-Wheels! This prayer-dimension is an essential feature of the way in which we pastorally care for other people. If prayer is

> The Christian's vital breath,
> The Christian's native air,

as James Montgomery's hymn puts it, we can't fulfil our responsibility without being ready to help here. We're not called upon to be very good at it (if we were, I shouldn't have the temerity to write about it at all); we are to recognize its basic importance, and to share what little we know with others, even if we ourselves still have to say, with the last line of the hymn,

'Lord, teach us how to pray.'

6

The Grey Areas

Boring, boring, boring . . . To some, part of the unattractiveness of the church lies in its sameness. They complain that there's little to be excited about, hardly anything fresh which takes you out of the monotonous services-routine. 'In the church,' as an ecclesiastical historian put it, 'it is always Monday, God's washing day, wiping away tears and washing away sins.' There, if only we could see it, is its real glory; and what is true of the church is also true of pastoral care. Nightdresses in the street aren't a common occurrence, and it will be but rarely that we're involved in anything dramatic or exciting. The more exotic and complex difficulties like drug abuse or alcoholism are agenda for the experts, even if there is considerable support we can offer to those closest to the victims themselves. Our pastoral care will largely be taken up with the unromantic, grey areas of life, those areas where there may not seem to be anything violently wrong, but where people feel anxious or empty, depressed or guilt-ridden; or where perhaps they may just be suffering from middle-age 'blues'. In all these areas, we need to be able to discern our limited but important role.

Anxiety

Freud made an important distinction between normal and neurotic *anxiety*. Normal fear is that common to us all which is anticipation of some future event, perhaps a crucial interview, a family confrontation or a surgical operation. Such fears can work to a person's advantage, for they can prepare them to cope with the practicalities of what is likely to happen – provided, of course, that they are not irrationally overwhelmed by their fears, and provided that they can find someone with whom to work through that preparation. It is here that our role is crucial. Our understandable first reaction is to confront the fear, and say that it shouldn't exist. We use comforting words about there being nothing to worry about, that many people have gone through the experience safely, and that in a few weeks' time our anxious friend will look back and wonder what all the fuss was about. We may go further and add a biblical quotation about 'the everlasting arms'. But you can't deny the reality of fear so easily. If it's true that it can have a positive value, then it lies in the way in which, together, the entire process which the fear inspires may be examined in detail beforehand, and then there can be a looking forward which doesn't have concealed within it unknown terrors. I have often found that anxious people can be helped to look at a range of possible repercussions, even 'the worst that could happen'. They then relax when they find that it is actually within their powers to cope. It may be that especially in those cases where an operation is to be faced, we can discover more information about it which the patient hasn't been able or doesn't want to find, and work through the information with him. That will give confidence, not only in us, but in the event itself, for the normal fear (which never leaves us) is fear of the unknown.

Some normal anxiety, then, can be used constructively in order to prepare realistically for what lies ahead. All of us are anxious at certain times, but most of us manage. However, much anxiety which we encounter will not be of this normal sort, but rather that which is neurotic. In this case, anxiety isn't necessarily related to the anticipation of a particular event, nor is it just a passing mood. Rather, it is like an unwelcome visitor who comes unannounced, and never leaves. There is a general feeling of foreboding, that something terrifying lies just round the corner, a perpetual sense of unease which sometimes reflects itself in physical symptoms. To other people, the anxieties may seem unreal, as if the person were bluffing – or simply weak-kneed – and we may find it difficult to be patient with them. I recall the number of times people have said to me, 'I could shake him', about someone in this state, and frequently we may feel moved to reach a judgment about the selfish obsession of the person concerned, especially when compared with the weight of starvation, homelessness, persecution and fatal illnesses which press on so many in the world. But in my experience, if we urge comparisons, exhortations, or even explanations, we drive them further into their misery, and make them run away from those of us who genuinely seek to help. We simply reinforce their feelings of guilt and inadequacy for being like this in the first place. Sometimes, of course, it is *we* who can't stand being in the presence of such gloom, feeling so helpless. It is often difficult to discern 'who is doing what to whom' in situations like this! And despite our helplessness, 'standing by' people in their state of neurotic anxiety, trying to go at *their* pace, rather than forcing them to accept the pace we'd like to move them to, is the most we can do. It is not for us to seek to *cure* them, however valuable the personal support we offer them, which in itself is therapeutic. We may have to urge them to seek both temporary alleviation, through tranquillizing drugs, and expert long-term psychiatric help. Incidentally, one difficulty we shall often encounter is the prejudice against receiving help from psychiatrists, which partly stems from the stigma attached to any suggestion of mental illness. But psychiatrists are our allies, potential liberators of the human spirit. No more than any other profession are they infallible, and, as many of them would be the first to admit, there is a lot yet to be learnt about the human psyche and its health. That means that, like the rest of us, they may be tempted by the short-cut answer that can be disastrously wrong in some cases, and they can sometimes fail to be able to help. But we shouldn't hesitate in recommending those who seem to need treatment to psychiatrists, whilst at the same time helping them to see that we seek to refer them not to ease *our* trouble but *theirs*, and that in no sense are they being abandoned.

Emptiness

An increasingly common experience, in my view, and typical of the 'grey areas of life', is that feeling of coldness or *emptiness* at the centre. It is as if for several people, life has lost its heart and point. It isn't that they're ill, or facing trying circumstances; indeed, in many cases, it often seems to be those for whom life is comfortable and without any major worries to whom this happens. Even the worthwhileness of religious faith, which perhaps they have never up to this point questioned, seems to desert them. Life becomes mechanical, almost a matter of shadow-boxing. When this has happened to people I know, I've often felt that it is because of someone, something, some one event which has caused them to stop and pause, and then reflect: not necessarily a crisis, or even something of which they've been very conscious. It is as if they've been on a fast-moving train with scenery flashing past at great speed, and the momentum of the journey has borne them along. Now the train has stopped. The various activities of life, getting on at work, bringing up a family, arranging the busy-ness of life, have until now given sufficient momentum to living; but now these are all looked at with some detachment. It is as though people going through this experience have never developed a still, rich centre which still holds when all the activities at the circumference stop, since it is not dependent on those activities, but exists of itself.

Situations like this are not patent of a quick or a uniform solution. This depends on helping people to discover within themselves the soil in which that still centre may grow. There's little doubt in my mind that the soil exists in us all, but it is fed and watered by different means, and it will be a slow growth. Someone I know was transformed, she felt, by opening her eyes and really looking for the first time at the shapes and colours in

the local park. She felt a great peace and a flooding back of life
at the centre as she contemplated the pattern of bare trees and
the sun playing through them on to the lake below. For others
it will be listening, rather than looking, and perhaps to that
music which is 'soul of man speaking to the soul of man'. Both
looking and listening are ways through which we can be taken
out of ourselves and immersed in a world which, in a curious
way, is beyond us and part of us at the same time. Another
means of nourishment is through the experience of open, loving
and relaxed relationships to be found in some groups and, we
trust, in many groups within the church. (Here it must be
stressed that the nourishment is indirect. Any attempt directly
to nourish is analogous to force-feeding, and is bound to and
deserves to fail. We belong, simply because it is good to belong,
and we enjoy other people, not because we're looking for a
result of our belonging. That would be fatal, and would spoil
the relationships themselves.) One other possibility is that of
taking on a small piece of voluntary work, such as visiting regularly one older person. Again, it is the business of being taken
out of the same circumstances which has produced the deadness
of spirit, the emptiness inside. Of course, the situation may bring
to the minds of some of us that well-known quotation from St
Augustine that we are made for God himself, and that our
hearts are restless until they rest in him. That is a profound
truth, and we may feel that we have sometimes, through our
own pain and heart-searching, stumbled on the truth of it for
ourselves. But like all profound truths, we need to grow into it:
it cannot be presented as a panacea or instant remedy for that
emptiness, which may have much to do with feelings about the
unreality of God, and his absence. It may be that not only has
there been death of worthwhileness elsewhere, but the death of
God, too. What then? I don't believe that the means of resolution are any different from that of which we have already
spoken. Truly to look, listen, love and care is to touch the hem
of God's garment, even if we never look up and make the connection between the garment and the wearer. Some in time will

look up, and perhaps come to see, dimly at first, his face, his gaze, his love. I have often found that line from Newman's hymn, 'And in the *depths* be praise', comforting and illuminating. It suggests that to those for whom all the traditional imagery of God has died, he may still be found in the depths of being, even deeper than the worst anxieties. Such reassurance is often to be found in the Psalms, a treasury of grace which captures every mood and phase of human existence.

Our job as carers is gently to make such suggestions as seem most likely to be helpful to the person concerned, and possibly to share the experience with them. If it is in looking and listening, it will be in silence, and silence shared can again powerfully point to that still rich centre for which we all seek. Shared silence is something which takes great courage to risk with someone, but it is sometimes fundamental. The quiet contrast to that feverish activity which has led to the feeling of emptiness is striking.

Failure

Allied to this feeling of emptiness is the feeling many of us have that we are *failures* as human beings. The very phrase is a contradiction in itself. It implies that we can be *successful* as human beings. To take two extremes to highlight the truth, we can be successful at many things. First, in getting to the top in our careers, in acquiring much wealth, in gaining popularity. None of these things necessarily means that we have become mature human beings in the process or achieved the goal towards which all humanity strives, the only way, that is, in which the word 'success' is applicable to human beings. Then, at the other end of the scale, when we seem to fail at everything we turn our hand to, and we slip tragically easily from 'failing at' to '*being* failures', we may have been able to begin to work through our failures, and see them as part of the maturing process – and that is success! After all, Christian faith has always known about defeat turned into victory, and tragedy becoming the source of hope.

This, it seems to me, is the attitude with which as pastoral carers we approach those who only see themselves as failures. Perhaps it's worth reflecting that if they have arrived at this stage of self-awareness, it is a stage further on than those who have been sheltering for years behind something which the psychologist calls the 'belonging-identity' (whether it be possessions, family or even organizations) to hide the truth of their 'failure' from themselves, to prevent them from becoming self-aware. To be able to face the truth about our own feelings without that sort of self-defensive prop is often hard-won, but it is great gain, and the first stage towards recovery. And whilst I profoundly believe what I have just been saying about 'success' and 'failure' as human beings, and indeed see it to be one of the keys to a more humane and caring society, we have to recognize the great pressures on all of us to be 'successful'. Despite the reaction and rebellion amongst many young people, the aims, standards and values of what has been called the 'achieving society', even from junior-school age, are still much with us. We value highly the skills required for success, whether it is the achievement of educational grades or adequate sexual performance. Even the church is infected: isn't the successful church seen as that which simply has a large congregation, flourishing activities, and a big financial turn-over?

However, once we begin to see that we are here not to achieve success, but to be human, we are released from a good deal of pretence and make-believe. I have a particular aversion to those annual duplicated letters dignified by the name of 'round robins' which purport to give you all news of the family over the past year. It isn't, I hope, that I am uninterested in the welfare of my friends and their children; it is that somehow, they seem to be so unreal in the promotions they've been given or number of 'O' and 'A' levels their children have acquired. Where are the failures we all have and know? Doesn't friendship actually mean that you can talk about them as well – with confidence? A clerical friend of mine once did a spoof 'round robin', in which he drew attention to 'grandmother having piles, John going on pot and Diana becoming pregnant at the age of sixteen'. Why aren't they ever like that? We needn't pretend that our marriages are the supremest of supreme successes, or that our children are the sparkling success they might be. We are all failures to some extent; what matters is the quality of love that is born out of our failure to be as good as we ought to be, as much as from being good itself. And when we see that, we have in a sense ceased to be failures, and ceased simply to see ourselves as failures.

Paradoxically, too (and here we touch once again the heart of pastoral care), it is often our failure to know how to help, our helplessness, our simple identification with others in their weakness and failure, that most helps other people – provided that we do not shirk the failure, or pretend that it isn't there. That is both demanding and liberating at one and the same time.

Guilt

There is one characteristic that is common to us all, very little talked about, and most deeply felt. I mean, of course, our *guilt-feelings*. I recall an agony columnist saying that the great majority of her letter-writers were plagued with guilt – about children, husbands, wives, parents, about their very existence – and I remember how our local radio station was flooded with calls when its late-night 'phone-in' programme centred on the subject of guilt. In my experience, guilt, spoken or unspoken, lies at the root of most situations presented by those who come for counselling.

As with anxiety, guilt-feelings have a positive and useful function. We feel guilty when we allow what we want to do to take the place of what we ought to do. And of course, if that didn't happen, if we always did what we wanted and never felt guilty, we should have a more desperate situation still. Guilt-feelings can make us responsible in our relationships with other people and prompt us to be reconciled with those we've hurt by our own thoughtlessness or carelessness.

But most guilt isn't like that: it's much more irrational. One lady said in all seriousness to me, 'I feel guilty because I don't seem to have anything to feel guilty about!' There was another lady I used to meet most mornings as she made her way to the station and I made mine to church. For months as we passed each other we just said, 'Good morning'; and then one day she stopped me and said, 'I wish I didn't meet you. All you do is smile and pass the time of day, and I always feel so guilty!' She then began to tell me how she knew she ought to go to church, but didn't – for a host of good reasons, as it turned out. That reminded me how in the church we can get people to do things they wouldn't otherwise do through manipulating their guilt-feelings; indeed, you can get people to do almost anything if you make them feel guilty enough about what they're enjoying at present. That is a very dangerous temptation for those of us in the church, who can always persuade ourselves that we're doing it for the best of ends.

Of course, the real role of the church is to release people from their guilt, not increase it. The mechanics of release through the appointed ways of confession and absolution, formally and informally, still exist, and are helpful to many. Perhaps one of the most urgent pastoral tasks of the church is to reassess those appropriate ways, to see how they can be of help to many more to whom at present they are nothing but an ecclesiastical routine. Nearly thirty years ago, the founder of the Iona Community argued for a recovery of the confessional in the Church of Scotland. He was appalled by the terrible fact that half the beds in mental hospitals are occupied by those who have an 'overloaded sense of guilt', and even more by 'the number of folk who will never see the inside of a mental home but who are living half lives because of an accumulated burden of sin'. He wasn't urging the obligation of confession, or what he called 'a return to birettas and cassocks or the egoistic strutting of doubtful authority'. He was, he said, searching for the focussing of forgiveness 'in the hands of the minister or sometimes in the

hands of an expert with peculiar gifts, be he clerical or lay, in
the midst of the congregation'.[1] The position has scarcely
improved in any church since George Macleod wrote those
words, and they may well stir some pastoral carers to take
initiatives to remedy a state of ignorance, prejudice and sad
inadequacy.

However the position improves, there will still be those who
don't or can't use the means of the confessional. How can we
help them as pastoral carers? Many of us hug our guilt to ourselves because we're deeply afraid that if we shared it with
someone else they'd cease to have as good an impression of us,
or even cease to love us. Parish priests find this to be true of
parishioners who sometimes prefer to go to confession elsewhere; the truth is that such are not thought any less of, but
rather more. I have heard counsellors operating in the secular
field argue that what they lack is some 'secular sacramental
act', whereby those whom they have helped are reintegrated
into ordinary relationship and shown outwardly that whatever
has been the nature of their 'confession', the counsellor's respect
for them as individuals is not diminished. An arm round the
shoulder scarcely seems adequate.

All this argues that if we're to help other people, we must be
the sort of people who can inspire such confidence that they're
able to feel that they can tell their full story to us. It isn't that
we must give an impression of perfection, or near-perfection,
but rather that we should reveal ourselves, too, as people who
have struggled, or are struggling, with matters unresolved in
our own lives. It will be our attempt to be unconditional, people
whose life doesn't depend on respectability, or on the other person's always doing what is right, with an openness and recep-
tivity which will draw people out, reassured by the knowledge
that our love will stay, whatever it is that the other person has
to tell us. I am not suggesting that we should encourage others
to parade their guilt, or wallow in it: few things are more
conducive to boredom in the listener and to self-pity in the
teller. I am indicating that we need to be those who encourage

the cause of guilt to be brought out into the open, and allow others to share their guilt with us. That sort of release, that draining-away of inner poison, is desperately important.

Depression

Anxiety (of both sorts) and emptiness, however difficult to live with, are states you might describe as being of partial eclipse. By contrast, the real state of depression, by which I don't mean a fluctuation of mood which includes feeling just a little under the weather, is a state of almost total eclipse. Confusion with the mood of feeling slightly depressed has meant that depression hasn't been understood for the total experience of blackness that it represents, and the result has been that the patient's suffering (I say patient, for depression in this sense is an illness) hasn't been taken as seriously as it might have been. Depression is a state of feeling utterly alone, on the edge of a black abyss, from which you can find no resources within you or without to organize an escape.

It has become common to talk of two types of depression – *endogenous*, which has its roots in the patient's personality or in his chemical balance or inbalance; and *reactive*, which arises as reaction to some external event, like the personal loss of a relative or friend or disappointment in promotion. This distinction is not exact, and recent research seems to indicate that depression is measurable along a scale of intensity, the differences relating to the strength of the depression rather than to its particular kind. Now clearly, since depression is an illness, expert medical and psychiatric help is necessary: Gerald Priestland, in describing his own depression, which he says needs a big 'D', says that he thanks God for modern drugs and psychiatry, and many of us have evidence of the way in which tranquillizing drugs have been a godsend (in the literal sense) to those suffering from depression. At the same time, we can't begin to cope with ourselves and with life generally by means of drugs, and continued use of drugs can prevent rather than help a person coming to terms with his own situation, because it can blur his sensitivity. It has recently been discovered that when two comparable groups of animals are subjected to experimental stress, those which are given no treatment develop a natural tolerance towards stress, and begin to adjust. On the other hand, those given anti-anxiety drugs do not develop this natural tolerance, and in the end are worse off, because they are locked into the anxiety state. This seems to indicate that drugs can drive human victims deeper into anxiety and dependence.

In addition to expert psychiatric help, or in the absence of it, there is a considerable contribution, therefore, which relatives and lay carers have to make to the welfare of a depressive. In my experience, it is the lack of any sense of self-worth which is his dominant characteristic, and it is often extremely wearisome for the one who stands by to have repeated over and over again the catalogue of feelings of hopelessness, misery, failure, despair and self-disgust. But we have to accept that the victim is suffering real pain, and his expressions of self-disgust do not necessarily come out of self-pity but out of great inner anguish. And the hardest part is the business of going on soaking up these painful feelings without trying to stop them or control them, or without using them to draw attention to the helper through parallels in his own life. To 'soak up' sounds merely passive; but really to listen and go on listening as such anguish gushes out is very exhausting; yet, in the end, it offers the best chance of healing. Often we may be tempted, and from the best of motives, to get religion to do what we can't do ourselves. But we need to recognize the ambiguity of religion at this point. Gerald Priestland says that for him religion only increased his sense of worthlessness and guilt; that illness deepened the chasm between himself and God; and that a sick mind could only conceive a sickened religion. And in my experience, it isn't only to the depressive that faith is of little help, and might even seem to make the sickness worse; it is also that a strong faith on the part of the helper might seem like a reproach, and increase guilt further. Consequently, any expression of the carer's faith may simply have to be in the way in which it informs and sustains the attitude of the carer. The word 'sustains' is a key-word, since perseverance to the end, the ability to go on giving of time and patience or, in a word, loving without counting the cost, is never more essential than in the case of the depressive. To withhold verbal expression of faith is very difficult for those to whom such expression comes naturally – but to withhold it out of love and care for the other person is a sign of greater faith still.

An important distinction is worth recognizing when we're tempted to 'use' religion as a means of therapy in cases like depression. It is valid in every sphere of religion and life, but particularly important when we're tempted to see religion as 'cure'. The researches of the psychologist Gordon Allport led him to ask the question why it was that 'on the average, church-goers are more bigoted towards minority groups than non-churchgoers', whilst some are leaders in the fight against ethnic prejudice. (The obvious example of Martin Luther King comes to mind.) Allport concludes that there are two basic types of religious orientation: one he calls extrinsic, the other intrinsic. Extrinsic religion is commitment to a faith that will serve your interests: it is something to use (for ceremony, family conveni-ence or personal comfort), but not to live. 'It may be used to improve one's status, to bolster one's self-confidence'; in short, it is 'a shield for self-centredness'. Intrinsic religion, on the other hand, 'is not instrumental. It is not a means of handling fear, a mode of sociability and conformity, a sublimation of sex or a wish-fulfilment. All these motives are somehow subordinated to an over-arching motive.' And that over-arching motive is the commitment of the whole person to the service of faith. 'Such religion does not exist to serve the person; rather the person is committed to serve it.'[2] It does not need much imagina-tion to see that it is only the latter, intrinsic faith, which provides some still centre of support in life's most anxious moments.

Those anxious moments often provide the test of the depth

and sort of a person's religious faith. It isn't only when we use religion as a cure that the extrinsic aspect shows itself, but whenever we make religion instrumental to our purposes, even when we see it chiefly as giving us hope, courage, resources to cope and so on. All these are by-products of a commitment, and the commitment is for its own sake.

So what is it that we as carers are offering to the depressive in our persevering work of absorbing his depression? Our very perseverance should help him finally not to lose hope and sink further into a pit of despair. He may come to feel that at least there is one person to whom, whatever he is like, he counts, and to whom he can relate, and that may enable him to modify his attitude towards other people as well. Since it is now agreed by many therapists of different schools of thought that depression is often frozen anger which a person turns back on himself instead of expressing, we may be able to encourage him to release that anger for us to absorb. (How often Christians run away from anger, rather than to try to absorb it!) One thing is certain: we can't jolly depressives out of their depression, and must not try. They cannot respond to that sort of warmth, and the nicer and pleasanter we try to be, the more depressed and anxious we make them. They can't cope with a friendliness which sometimes seems overdone, and false heartiness can post-pone their recovery. On the other hand, there are several prac-tical things we can encourage, over appearance, about diet and in encouraging the depressive to accomplish some small task which is within his range, and which will partially restore for him his self-esteem when he finds that he can be effective to that small degree.

In the end, there is no substitute for that loving relationship which will assure him that come what may, he will never be deserted, that in all the surrounding darkness there is a warm hand and just a pin-point of light. Sometimes that relationship will be expressed in shared silence: just being quiet with the depressed, since like those who are bereaved, they may really be beyond the reach of words.

Suicide

The word *suicide* is likely to raise a flutter of panic in many of us. (Remember the nightdress in the street, again.) That makes doubly important cool consideration of the question, as a preparation for any experience we may have. There is one important and neglected factor we especially need calmly to explore. Psychology and Christian faith, as we have seen, come together in agreeing that life is about the growth of human beings to maturity, and that that maturity consists of the business of making choices and accepting responsibility for them. We become fully ourselves through our moral choices. But if the real choice is the essence both of morality and maturity, then why not choice *here*, over the question of whether to die or not as well as in the myriad choices in life?

It isn't only our instinctive obligation to preserve life at all costs or the Christian insistence on the sanctity of life, even though the New Testament is very silent in condemnation of suicide, which prevents us from following the full implications of choice in human life to its logical conclusion. It is that, excepting some martyrs and Captain Oates going out into the blizzard, we find it difficult to think of a death that has been chosen as being in any sense honourable, as being the considered outcome of a total reflection on circumstances and issues. Yet we can all think of situations, certain illnesses, physical handicaps or emotional upheavals where we might wish to choose to die, where we might conclude that it would be better for the people and causes and institutions we hold dear if we were not around any more. And if we think of our lives as being in some way analogous to works of art, not to be spoilt by the introduction of material which is alien to the picture, and which cannot be integrated with the whole, then, bizarre though it sounds, suicide may complete the picture. I think that I have known two people whose suicides were the fruit of an agonizing reflection on what was in the best interests of all concerned and, not least, of the completeness of their own lives. And I

believe that a society which is on the road to maturity will
increasingly recognize and salute the responsibility of choice.

Now, of course, if that were all to be said, I could rightly be
accused of talking simply (if not naively) on a lofty plane of
ethical idealism, a Utopia of the distant future, rather than the
messy relativities in which we are always immersed. But I've
tried to isolate this matter of choice in order to try and lay bare
the central issue, which so often gets hidden, and the implications of which we do not yet know how to handle. The truth is
that, as with every other moral and ethical question, we can't
turn up the easy answer in the back of the book, even the books
of scripture. Suicide is a term that covers many different acts,
widely varying in their moral quality. I have heard psychiatrists advance the dogma, without argument, that all suicides or
suicide attempts are the result of diagnosable illness, which is a
very convenient dogma since it neatly disposes of all moral
questions which might be involved. Most of us will not be so
easily satisfied, and will need to go on wrestling with the messy
relativities. Clearly, some suicides seem to be the result of
psychological compulsion, and can therefore be subject to moral
judgment; some are actions which could technically be termed
suicide, but which, if we were sufficiently courageous, we would
see as being worthy of moral approval; some would seem simply
to be cowardly and selfish; some we shall never understand.

For us as pastoral carers there may be two questions we need
to keep in mind and – if we are granted the suitable opportunity
– to pose. The first is to be as certain as possible that the depressed person is not simply acting under the impulse of a mood,
and has seriously been helped to consider possibilities for the
future; the second is whether the effect of his suicide on others
for whom he most cares has been carefully weighed. Choice is
crucial; but we never exercise choice in a vacuum, and choice
must always be made in the context of the welfare of others as
well as ourselves – and perhaps, too, of the loss of any general
or particular contribution we might make to the welfare of
society as a whole. The guilt heaped on those closest to the

person who commits suicide is often enormous, and in many cases, it is guilt no more deserved by them than it is by the rest of us bound together in a network of human relationships which is often indifferent and uncaring.

I think there are twin dangers for us as we seek to care when there is a possibility of suicide: that of not taking it seriously enough and that of taking it too seriously. In the first case, our coolness may push the other person closer to the brink because it may be perceived not as coolness but as that emotional indifference of other people which caused the misery in the first place. In the second case, our judgment will be clouded by our sense of panic, and the clear-headedness which would be one of our chief assets will depart. So we will not try to cajole depressed persons out of suicide or use every artifice to distract them in some activity outside themselves. Nor will we, and this is a great temptation to good Christians, use Christian and church arguments to try to dissuade them, or worse still, threaten with the consequences of eternal punishment. We shall keep as closely and fully as possible to the two questions. Sometimes we may find it helpful to be allowed to admit that we have at some time or another considered suicide; without triggering off condemnation or panic in the listener, this can be very significant in breaking the ice-cool ring which shuts them off from relationship. And we shall also recognize that on several occasions we shall be in touch with people whose talk of suicide is a bid for relationship, a cry for help. It isn't safe, as statistics show, to assume that it's only those who don't talk about it who commit suicide, but we shall almost certainly be involved with those who over-dramatize their situation in their desperate search for solace.

I recognize that the practical problems with which suicide leaves us are immense, and that even to write about them at all is somehow to trivialize them. But as pastoral carers, we can help, though it's a slow process, to make more opportunities for freer choice without the crippling effects of guilt and failure in us all. My own experience tells me that suicide is more connected with a loss of a sense of self-worth than it is with anything we do; and (I necessarily repeat myself) that sense of self-worth is only indirectly attained by the way other people value us. I find it hard to take that a society which allows for so much devaluation of persons, and consequently pushes some in the direction of self-destruction, should at the same time multiply the guilt with which other people have to live, once that act of suicide has taken place.

7

The Boundaries of Life

Attempts to portray pastoral care can lead to a major misunder-
standing. They can indirectly suggest that all that is necessary
is that we *do* certain things aright, put certain rules into practice, as it were. I recently came across a list of no less than fifty
'dos' and 'don'ts' which we all need to observe in visiting the
sick – including some warnings about knocking before entering
the room and not chewing gum or picking our teeth! The
realistic truth is that even when we observe all the rules (and
many of them are sound common sense), we may still be of little
help. It is the quality of the meeting between two people which
counts more than anything else, what we are able to give of our
own resources to the other, and in giving, also to receive.

In a long poem, the Cornish poet, Charles Causley, vividly
portrays ten types of hospital visitor: they are illuminating
pieces of self-examination.[1]

> The first enters wearing the neon armour
> Of virtue.
> Ceaselessly firing all-purpose smiles
> At everyone present
> She destroys hope
> In the breasts of the sick,
> Who realize instantly
> That they are incapable of surmounting
> Her ferocious goodwill
>
> Such courage she displays
> In the face of human disaster!

Fortunately, she does not stay long.
After a speedy trip round the ward
In the manner of a nineteen-thirties destroyer
Showing the flag in the Mediterranean,
She returns home for a week
– With luck, longer –
Scorched by the heat of her own worthiness.

We can all be so overpowering in our good deeds, so full of
all-embracing, all-devouring good will that instead of coming
close to others in their pain or misery we can enclose them more
firmly in it. Only a proper reticence, which is not hesitation but
self-effacement, will give the patient confidence to come out
close to us. It is a deadly temptation to smother other people's
griefs and miseries, not allowing any part of them to come out –
and nothing smothers more than heartiness. And in the end,
we're helping whom? Ourselves. We're fanning the flames of
'our own worthiness'. Quite unconsciously, under the guise of
good works to others, we're feeding our own egotism.

The second appears, a melancholy splurge
Of theological colours;
Taps heavily about like a healthy vulture
Distributing deep-frozen hope.

The patients gaze at him cautiously.
Most of them, as yet uncertain of the realities
Of heaven, hell-fire, or eternal emptiness,
Play for safety
By accepting his attentions
With just-concealed apathy,
Except one old man, who cries
With newly sharpened hatred,
'Shove off! Shove off!
'Shove . . . . shove . . . . shove . . . . shove
Off!
Just you
Shove!'

We may, of course, think that we're doing good deeds and also taking care of the patient's eternal salvation (whether they're interested or not). To dangle religious 'certainties' before those to whom all religious language is dead language is to use them as objects rather than as subjects, a denial of Christian faith in itself. Many will be too polite to resist – and the warmest feeling that in the weakness of their captivity they'll be able to show is apathy. To be told to 'shove off' is a highly moral, because honest response . . .

> The third skilfully deflates his weakly
> > smiling victim
> By telling him
> How the lobelias are doing,
> How many kittens the cat had,
> How the slate came off the scullery roof,
> And how no one has visited the patient for
> > a fortnight
> Because everybody
> Had colds and feared to bring the jumpy
> > germ into hospital.
>
> The patient's eyes
> Ice over. He is uninterested
> In lobelias, the cat, the slate, the germ.
> Flat on his back, drip-fed, his face
> The shade of a newly dug-up Pharaoh,
> Wearing his skeleton outside his skin,
> Yet his wits as bright as a lighted candle,
> He is concerned only with the here, the now,
> And requires to speak
> Of nothing but his present predicament.
>
> It is not permitted.

This is a classic case, and so typical. Endless small talk and chatter, we feel, will divert the patient's attention, and make

him feel better, more interested in 'something other than themselves'. That, in certain circumstances, may be well justified;
but the patient knows it for what it is – an escape from an entering into *his* or *her* situation, a scratching of the surface, rather
than a willingness to enter the deeps, where it hurts most.
Nothing will help the patient more, give him more release, than
to be allowed to speak of his present predicament. And 'it is not
permitted'. Why? Again, not for the patient's sake – but for the
protection of the helper, who finds the business of going there
too threatening, too demanding.

> The sixth visitor says little,
> Breathes reassurance,
> Smiles securely,
> Carries no black passport of grapes
> And visa of chocolate. Has a clutch
> Of clean washing.
>
> Unobtrusively stows it
> In the locker; searches out more.
> Talks quietly to the Sister
> Out of sight, out of earshot, of the patient.
> Arrives punctually as a tide.
> Does not stay the whole hour.
>
> Even when she has gone
> The patient seems to sense her there:
> An upholding
> Presence.

That says it all: 'an upholding presence'. But notice how the
upholding presence goes with an intense practicality and sensitivity to real needs – clean linen, punctuality, a wish not to tire
the patient. And both presence and practicality seem to come
from a faith which doesn't need noise, words ('says little') or
conventional gifts to give confidence either to helper or to
patient. Sometimes shy people, even friends, may need 'small

talk' as stepping-stones to reach each other at first – so long as they are stepping-stones, and not evasive pathways. For the greatest resource we have is the faith, forged in the darkness of Calvary, that ultimately nothing, however dark it seems at the moment, will or can separate us from God's love. And it is our *attitude* which conveys that, not any self-conscious desire to witness.

I can testify to the truth of Charles Causley's descriptions. On looking back to two recent spells in a men's hospital ward, I contrast two visits, one from an agnostic, and one from a clergyman. The agnostic hates hospitals and finds the sight of blood or the story of operations too painful to bear. He only stayed five minutes, but I knew what it had cost to come at all, and he did what was the most helpful thing anyone could have done there – left me some ten-penny pieces for the travelling 'phone. I contrast that experience with the visit I endured from an earnest clergyman who made it plain that he thought he was doing his duty, wearied me with a long account of what he'd been up to in a church conference the previous week, prayed with me in formal fashion, and had an afterthought after he'd said goodbye and had started to walk down the ward: 'Is there anything you want?'

Supposing it isn't a sick-room or general hospital bed we're visiting: suppose it is someone who is known to be dying, a terminal-care patient? Here, obviously, many of the fears and inhibitions and hesitations we feel in general visiting will still be present, though intensified; here, too, a combination of presence with practicality is even more important.

It is hard on everybody's part to resist negative feelings in working with dying people. It is but natural that often a dying patient spells failure to the doctor and a sense of pathetic hopelessness and helplessness to others. And we're all working against the remnants of a death-denying culture which makes it illegitimate to face the question with any degree of openness. It is often said that when we look at someone known to be dying, we look at them as if they are already dead. Here the Hospice

Movement has been largely responsible for a minor revolution
in attitudes. It has become possible to see the time between the
acknowledgment of the probability of death (barring a miracle,
which can never be ruled out) and the death itself in a positive
way, as providing the opportunity for integration, completion.
Again, it is the quality of life that matters, not the short amount
of time, and it is to do with the recognition of the blessedness of
the boundary of death, the line which it draws. The universal
testimony of those who have been given notice of a few months
to live seems to be a new appreciation of the wonder of each
day, a fresh 'seeing' of things previously unnoticed. The explicit
recognition of the frontier-line gives a sense of worth-whileness
to all that happens. Endless existence without the rhythm of the
changing seasons of life would deprive life of a lot of colour and
meaning. Once we can embrace this truth, then it is possible to
begin to transform a negative view of death – and also to see
death as the last stage of growth. It is significant that in the
Hindu tradition the fourth and final phase of a life which is
rounded is the phase of 'letting go', and this is most dramatically
shown by those who go to the River Ganges and want to die in a
manner which achieves liberation and salvation. A merely negative approach to death robs us of the chance to see life rounded
and whole – whenever death occurs. It isn't too fanciful or
unreal to see each human life as a work of art which death
completes. In the Jerusalem Bible translation St Paul actually
tells the Ephesians that 'we are God's work of art'. That isn't to
deny (as certain religious traditions insist) that beyond death
growth continues until we're fit for the nearer presence of God.
But it does something to restore that necessary sense of wholeness and significance to each individual, which we've so much
lost in our fragmented world, and which it is one of the privi-
leges of pastoral care to insist upon. It's easy to be misunderstood here: as if we should be ready to welcome death all too
easily and quickly, and consequently, devalue human life here,
or as if we are making a bid for the revival of the Victorian
obsession with death. I am not denying the incompleteness, the

frustrations, the unfulfilled longings which constitute much of human life this side of death, or the hope for the resolution of all these things beyond death. Error creeps in when that resolution is seen as the only factor which makes sense of this life, for it is to do less than justice to God's creation, and the resultant affirmation of life which every Christian must make.

So the last stage of life, even when death is known to be near, is significant. To me, an unforgettable scene was that of a lady having her hair permed in a hospice on the day before she died: even at the extreme hour, her dignity as a person mattered. Now you may wonder at the relevance of this almost philosophical excursion into death and its meaning in considering pastoral care. There is a real connection. 'Being there', the fundamental in all our care for the dying, implies that we won't seek to avoid close contact with dying and death, that we can stand it, bear it. But to be able to do that means that we shall have to come to terms with the inner conflict which such close contact nearly always involves. We shall, that is, have faced the certainty of our own death realistically, and that will unconsciously help the patient more than anything else to live with the threatening fact of his own impending death. Conversely, any inner conflict which still remains will leave an adverse effect on any to whom we seek to minister. A parallel with being unable to cope with being near someone dying because we haven't come to terms with our own death is that of being unable to be alongside someone with depression if we have not begun to come to terms with our own feelings of worthlessness and purposelessness. The recognition of the 'blessedness of the boundary of death' is an important factor in the business of coming to terms with death. I am not for a moment suggesting any absolutes, as if any of us will come to terms fully – as in all pastoral care, it is that towards which we are *tending*. And whether we like it or not, or say anything or not, we communicate our hopes and anxieties to other people.

It may be helpful sometimes to identify the various stages through which a patient has to go if he is going to adjust to the process of dying. Experts have identified five such stages: denial, isolation, anger, bargaining (which moves into depression) and acceptance. There may be variations in the length of each stage, and there isn't necessarily gradual or uninterrupted progress from one to the other.

Denial ('I'll be back at work before long') may be to protect himself or his relatives from the impact of the shock: it is a defence-mechanism which allows him still the possibility of hope, and the ability to begin to adjust to it.

Isolation ('You don't know what it's like: I have to go through it myself') is the intense loneliness which gradual recognition of the condition brings, which may be heightened if carers bring into it much of their own anxieties about death.

Anger is the next response: 'Why should it happen to me?' The angry mood reinforces any natural inclination we have to avoid the patient, because it is hard to endure, just at the point where he most needs befriending.

The bargaining phase is the point at which the patient seems to be beginning to come to terms with his own death, but on conditions. (I wouldn't mind so much – *if only* . . .' It's the 'if only' which is the most common phrase.)

The bargaining phase can slip into *depression* ('Nothing does any good'). It is now that there is the greatest temptation to play the part of 'cheering up', again diverting his attention from his real and pressing situation to something else which we feel will comfort and placate him.

Acceptance ('You know I'm going, don't you?') is the final stage, in which the patient has begun to make his own preparation for death, when he seems ready to let go, the arrival of a stage which may be conveyed through a smile, or touch, when words may be difficult. Meeting with the experience of death is a lone meeting: that is its glory, which again confers significance on the person – but it is also its dread. And that gives us a clue to what it is that we can best offer: that we will go with them to the end, that they will not be left unsupported, abandoned. Often this will best be achieved through touch. For those patients who have gone beyond the reach of our words, it is our touch which will assure them they're not deserted. And incidentally, the way we sit with or stand by the patient speaks volumes for the way in which we're prepared to be involved – or not. Again, the Hospice Movement has taken away the false sting of death by giving assurance to the patient that their pain will always be controlled, and never get out of hand, and that at no time will they be forsaken, that they can approach their end in a manner consonant with the dignity of any human being, whoever they are.

So our care for dying people is directed towards helping them to live until they die rather than just preparing them for death. We shall almost certainly be brought up against the question – should the patient be told that he is going to die? Most of us would wish to strive for a situation in which patient and relatives are aware rather than living in a dishonest 'conspiracy of silence' (perhaps deception would be a better word) so that fears can properly be expressed on both sides and real communication is possible. Few situations are more ludicrous than those in the middle of which I have sometimes found myself, when the relatives aren't telling the patient because he couldn't stand it, and the patient isn't letting on to the relatives because 'they'd be so upset!' But it can't simply be right to insist always on telling all, willy-nilly. A person's approach is unique to that person. And the actual and full circumstances of a person's attitude to life must be taken into consideration. If, for example, a person has previously not been able to look death in the face, and studiously avoided it, then the difficulty of helping him to come to terms with it is immeasurably increased. And any violent tearing away of the patient's defence can't possibly be right; indeed, it may even be right (at least temporarily) to support the defence-mechanism, since it is the one real resource the patient has for coping, and if that goes, there is nothing on which to fall back. That is a sure recipe for final hopelessness and despair. Of course, there must always be kept open the possibility of change; and for some, death really can be the final stage of growth, as we've seen. But very often in our pastoral care we shall be supporting weakness which started in problems stretching back a long way into the patient's earlier life – problems which might have been resolved then, but which have hardened into a permanent attitude to life. It is too late to begin to resolve those problems and modify attitudes in terminal care. My conviction is that it is *how* people are told any truth about their condition which matters most. Nurses working in terminal care often have the experience of being asked the question 'Am I going to die?' at the most inconvenient of moments, often, for instance, when their physical and emotional resources are at a low ebb, perhaps at two-o'clock in the morning. The guide-line is telling as much truth as it is thought the patient can bear with gentleness and care, but always with the assurance that they will never be abandoned, or left unaided to cope with some physical crisis that emerges.

Life is a succession of small bereavements: we are losing all the time. So unlike the process of dying, into which we have not yet entered, but simply done our best to come to terms with the fact, the process of bereavement is something of which we all have knowledge. I have already mentioned the steps of bereavement which have been identified by people like Colin Murray Parkes and others, in particular the first stage of *numbness and shock*, and the support appropriate to it. To complete the picture, the second stage is the stage when there may be intense feelings of *yearning* for the dead person; feelings of anger with the doctors, the hospitals – and even paradoxically, with the deceased himself for having left the bereaved 'like this'; feelings of guilt begin to emerge as there is plenty of time to look back on what the bereaved did or failed to do. Post-bereavement guilt can become a most intractable problem, in that there is no one to whom one can make reparation, and outside a religious framework of confession and forgiveness there is no obvious mechanism with which to deal with the problem. Here, above all, it is necessary that we share the pain and grief, which shouldn't be avoided. But not to be afraid to show your true

feelings means that there must be someone to whom those feelings can be shown, someone who will above all listen when the
bereaved does that which may be most necessary, talk about
the deceased. The second stage shades into the third stage of
aimlessness and *disorientation*, when very often nothing seems important and worthwhile to the bereaved. But that stage, when
the real situation and the necessity for readjustment is beginning to be apparent, is a transitional stage to that (almost
comparable to 'rebirth') when the bereaved begins to come
through to the final stage of *acceptance*. Then he may begin to
see that, whatever his religious faith, the bereavement is not
total loss, and that the deceased has become part of him. He
will begin to see that he is a different person because of the
relationship, and that in itself ensures that there will be no
final separation.

These identifiable stages in the process of grieving must not
be taken as fitting every experience, nor must we try to put
everybody into the framework of the various stages. Too much
reliance on the framework may mean that we will miss the
particular significance of something that is happening in someone's life. What is helpful is to know that in general, the
bereaved go through these stages, with varying depths of intensity, and different time-spans. It will mean that we will be
able to reassure members of the bereaved's family that the
reactions to grief which the bereaved may be suffering are not
abnormal – and will eventually pass. Simply to help a person
know that what is happening is part of what happens to us all
often gives great relief and support. In bereavement, as in other
emotional crises, I have found people take immense strength
and encouragement from the fact that to the listener what they
are experiencing and expressing 'hangs together'. To be reassured of this takes the panic out of the experience, and the fear
that some mental disturbance is taking place. Of course, the
quiet Christian hope of eternal life can be a great sustaining
power in bereavement – but it cannot and must not be treated
as a *substitute* for the grieving-process, through which we all,

Christians and others, need to go. Sometimes good Christians have been made to feel guilty if they express grief – as if they were lacking in faith – and that makes the process all the harder to bear.

There are two groups of people to whom bereavement can be an especially difficult experience. Often older people suffer the loss of their partner just at the time when their contemporaries are leaving them one by one, and their loss is made more stark by a feeling of increasing isolation. Younger and middle-aged people are often faced not only with many practical problems, and the bringing up of children single-handed, but with the avoidance-techniques others employ, and subsequent exclusion from social events since they now constitute an embarrassment. I recall a widow saying to me that being no longer part of a 'socially accepted couple' was one of the hardest things she had to cope with as a widow – and one of the longest-lasting.

In the process of bereavement our task as pastoral carers will be directed towards allowing the bereaved our time and space and confidence properly to grieve, nor will we intrude upon it, or attempt to make them act differently. We are, in the end, developing an atmosphere which helps all concerned to understand what is going on, and respond to it. That means being available not only to the bereaved himself, but also to the various members of the family who will also be affected by the grieving-process. To have someone outside the family, with a proper sense of detachment and involvement, who is at hand to absorb the necessary demonstrations of pain and loss, is an incalculable resource.

8

Ourselves as Carers

What of ourselves, as carers? Once we see the priority of lay caring and once we are enlisted in the army of 'carers', then we may suffer the delusion that the world can be divided into two sorts: the carers and the cared-for. Nothing could be more destructive for both, or more unreal. Whether we are 'active carers' or not, we are cared for, and sometimes and paradoxically by the cared for! All caring relationships are mutual. Both partners support each other and learn from each other. Even when we are involved in caring for a patient who is dying, we are gaining from their experience that which will come to support us when we face our own experience of dying. You don't need to be the member of a church for long to realize that hard-and-fast distinctions between church and world are unrealistic, and it is equally true of pastoral care. It is no bad thing, when we are brought to the first steps of pastoral care, to look at ourselves and examine as honestly as we can what it is *in us* that is pulling us in this direction. I recall great damage being done by a well-intentioned married lady without children who smothered the boys of a Bible class in consequence of her maternal deprivation – and she didn't begin to recognize the truth of the situation. The greater our enthusiasm for caring, the more clear we need to be about our motives. Of course, none of us is going to get it right, see ourselves with devastating clarity, be purged of all self-regarding motives, shut out our own needs as we concentrate exclusively on the needs of others. It is recognition of our mixed motivations which matters; and only that recognition will save us from adopting an attitude of implied superiority or even an artificial pose. There will often be occasions when those of us who are carers will feel weak, inadequate, vulnerable, even more in need of help than those we're supposed to be helping! What, then, do we do? We can deny our feelings of frailty, put a brave front on it, maintain a show of strength. And there's a strong presumption on us to do just that, to say that we feel what we feel we ought to feel! This is a characteristic Christian trap. We are not often encouraged to admit negative feelings to ourselves, let alone to other people. But it prevents us from being real, and there are occasions when being real, and disclosing weaknesses and inadequacies, is the necessary catalyst in a caring situation. The gap between the carer and the cared-for, as perceived by the latter, may be so great, in certain crisis situations where some form of counselling is being offered, that only some such admission, or some recognition of common humanity will enable a breakthrough to occur.

I am suggesting that the more relaxed we are about ourselves, the more whimsical and sceptical we are about our own motivation, the better carers we shall be. In my more mischievous moods, in the midst of many earnest discussions about being 'useful', I sometimes feel like protesting our 'uselessness', since it is the 'uselessness' of being which may accomplish more than much 'useful' doing, and bring a little warm humanity to what we are. We can go further. Carl Gustav Jung, surely a professional amongst professionals, used to say that if he wanted to treat a patient psychologically, he had to give up all pretensions to authority or superior knowledge, or any wish to influence. How many of us are prepared to be in a caring situation as defenceless, unconditional, helplessly exposed as that? But only that sort of relationship is real, and if there is a difference between the carer and the cared-for it may only be the difference between one who has been prepared to jettison all pretences and defences and one who is still hidden behind them both. The deadly enemy of caring is earnestness, that humourless determination which wants you to hand over the running of

your life to them on the grounds that they know best. And even
if they did, it would be an inadequate reason for making such
a handover. It is very sad when well-intentioned, blameless
characters, innocent of anything but 'your good', are frustrated
in their good works because their very earnestness proves an
obstacle to other people, and far from encouraging them to seek
help, makes them withdraw still further. ('I can tell by the look
in your eye that you're determined to help me!')

Now it might almost sound as if I'm advocating a degree of
indifference or lack of commitment in our carer. Not a bit of it.
Earnestness, gritting one's teeth in self-endeavour, is ultimately
a sign of a certain absence of faith, rather than its presence; it
is to be persuaded that if I don't do it, no one else will, and that
consequently not only the other person, but God himself, cannot manage without me. But other people are not in our hands
but in his. Of course, some emergencies will arise, in which we
shall need to act with intense concentration and resolution, but
even there we need to recall the client in the nightdress, rushing
out into the street – and not be frightened or perturbed. 'To
care and not to care' *properly* is a lesson to be learnt, and it is a
lesson in faith.

What, then, do we need? What resources will enable us to
keep our sensitivity in our caring? Our discussion of our mixed
motives for caring quite clearly highlights one resource we all
need: to be able to open ourselves up to another person in whom
we have complete trust, who can help us assess our motives, for
instance, who knows us well enough to see what is really going
on inside us. Some of us may be fortunate enough to have a
friend, whether a member of the church or not, who will be
ready and willing to do this for us. But assume for a moment
that that is not the case. What are the implications for the
church as a local community of carers? Ought it not to provide
just that sort of resource, that level of personal involvement
with each other? Recently, a question that has received some
attention in the helping professions is, 'Who helps the helpers?'
Is the high suicide-rate amongst psychiatrists at least partly

attributable to the way in which involvement in other people's dilemmas at a deep subconscious level shows up the chaos in their own personal lives, a chaos which isn't, for professional reasons and reasons of confidentiality, able to be shared with other people? Where do social workers with heavy case-loads find release and sources of refreshment and renewal? Does there exist a structure of pastoral care in our churches, especially those who pride themselves having bishops as pastors, which enables clergymen and ministers to be freed from the isolation their position often seems to impose, and gives them a real chance to speak of their own fears, frustrations and loneliness? From my own limited experience in the Anglican church, the answer to the last question is sadly negative. But what is a body of carers about if it doesn't mutually share in the caring, if people don't care for one another? And if my assumption that the church is such a community of carers is right, then what does this presuppose for the organization of church-life?

It partly means a focus on the small group, small enough for slow and patient talking or listening, but always alert to the dangers of introversion and excessive cosiness. It almost certainly will entail shared silence; this is such a difficult and sometimes painful experience, even if rewarding in the end, that it takes a long time to develop. It might, also, sound strange in the ears of those who see the church atmosphere in terms of busy services, or service. But one example of what I mean could be found in the work of the Companies of the movement which came to be known as Servants of Christ the King, founded by Roger Lloyd.[1] In their meetings, members shared in half-an-hour's corporate silence on a theme of 'common concern' and shared their reflections on that theme, each person in turn, finally deciding what practical action, if any, should be taken by the group. Clearly, this may be very relevant for some tasks of pastoral caring that the group undertakes together. But there is no reason why the 'common concern' in a flexible group shouldn't be that which is uppermost in the minds of each member, so that real 'sharing, caring' cooperation can take place. Some members of the group will know more than others about the particular people or concerns being spoken of. Of course, such groups demand a high degree of confidence in one another, and confidentiality in handling their material. Those two qualities must be part of a rich church life which takes pastoral care seriously, and I have seen from different examples in different places that this is not only possible, but yields to the members a satisfaction and depth of living which is a pearl of great price. It is naturally important that the establishment of such small groups shouldn't create the wrong impression: for instance, that only those who are in them are taking pastoral care seriously or that you can't be a 'pastoral carer' without that support. It can't be too strongly emphasized that there are diversities of pastoral care as there are diversities of gifts which God bestows on us. What is important is the opportunity we're given to share in our caring concern, and that has been all too tragically missing from the life of the church in general for far too long. If caring were just about 'practical matters', for bustling, zealous, breathless disciples, then it wouldn't matter: but since caring is as much a matter of the mind and emotions as it is of the will-to-serve, then it matters a great deal that an outlet for quiet thought, sharing in concern together, reflection on action, is always available. And lest that again creates an impression of over-seriousness and furrowed brows, it should be stressed that the value of such a group will be to take some of the heat out of the common problems, to help people to laugh together and relax.

That brings us to a characteristic danger of all pastoral caring. Inevitably, most of our caring is to do with the negative side of life, offering support in and through times of personal crisis, and we may begin to assume that Christian concern is only with such areas of life. Dietrich Bonheoffer, looking from his prison cell at the way Christian faith shows itself in the world, realized the danger: 'God must be recognized at the centre of life, not when we are at the end of our resources; it is his will to be recognized in life, and not only when death comes; in health

and vigour, and not only in suffering; in our activities, and
not only in sin.'²

The inherent difficulty for full-time and professional carers
is that their time is so taken up with the 'ambulance' side of
life that it is sometimes impossible to keep a balance. Life becomes distorted, and the temptation is simply to seek release
through the artificial escapism afforded by drink and drugs.
Lay pastoral carers are much more bound up with different
life-experiences; their other involvements prevent such distor-
tion. Even so, any concentration on the negative side of life
tends to make us believe that God is to be found only in and
through suffering. This so colours our attitude that we are less
effective than we might be, for those who are beset by problems
inevitably see their problems and the solution of them as being
the key to the whole of life, and their and our intentness can
squeeze out the possibility of beauty, trust, spontaneity and fun.
They need to be in touch with just that dimension, and it is our
'wholeness' as carers which will ensure it. The attitude of 'I'm
a carer; you can soon see if you look at my furrowed brow and
worried expression' needs to be dispelled. Of course, the opposite
of that, the perpetual, grinning expression which continually
invites you to cheer up, is equally unhelpful. The characteristic Christian quality of joy is neither; it is independent of
time and circumstance, doesn't necessarily arise as the successful outcome of a particular event, but is nourished by an underlying faith in God's love whatever the circumstances, and can
from time to time bubble over spontaneously. In the New
Testament, joy often occurs in the context of suffering and
separation. It was for the joy that was set before him, we're
told, that Jesus endured the cross, and it was when he was
speaking of his own going away that he also said, 'No one shall
rob you of your joy.'³ Abraham Maslow discovered through his
research that one important factor contributing to the maturity
of people was frequent experience of this spontaneous 'bubbling-
over'. But we can develop neither the steady flame nor the
'peak-experiences' of joy merely by willing them, or wishing

them. The flame glows as we nurture our faith in God's love; the 'peak-experience' comes uninvited, and the most we can do is to be sensitive to it, to be ready to realize it and let it do its work for us. Like happiness, joy is a by-product which flows from a sense of the worthwhileness and the wholeness of life – and it is a surprise.

Pastoral carers, then, will be open to the experience of joy, not only on their own account, but also because joy is an important quality which the 'cared-for' will sense in the carer for the sake of his own recovery and health. To speak directly of joy to someone in the grip of misery or despair would be cruel; to be able to communicate joy indirectly is to open the door of hope for another person, the hope that out of the present concentration on distress a new wholeness will emerge.

Joy, then, cannot be sought directly; but there is an important way of preparing for it, and it is to do with giving ourselves time to appreciate unhurriedly experiences open to us. The more we give of our time and energy and concentration to other people, the more time we need by ourselves – and this may well be misunderstood as selfishness. Perhaps it seems absurd to suggest that there could even be such space for leisure in lives which are already so committed to pastoral care, and I'm not only asking the question which the poet asks about the life 'full of care' in which 'we have no time to stand and stare'. I'm suggesting that the 'standing and staring' – perhaps at a scene from nature, in snow or sunlight, perhaps at a painting, perhaps at the faces of children as they play – enriches us, and hence enriches our caring. Properly to *see* people is an indispensable aspect of pastoral care, and very often our care is most valuable when it is extended to those who would otherwise be unnoticed.

That brings us to the heart of the matter: the spiritual resources we have to nourish us, and the link between our prayers and our worship in church and our caring. Of course, the seeing we have just mentioned can be part of our prayer, for prayer is that which holds our attention, gives us a sense of mystery, beauty, design and wonder. The point at which caring

most obviously touches our prayer is our intercession, our hold-
ing individuals in love in the presence of God. That is different
from petitionary prayer as commonly understood, which is to
make a specific petition in the faith that what we think is in
the best interest of the person should be granted by God. There
are occasions when such petitionary prayer is valid. But many
more will the occasions be when, as it were, we are directing an
'arrow prayer' at God's heart without presuming to tell him
what he should do about it! (I've always thought that the
Authorized Version of Mary and Martha's message to Jesus
about Lazarus is a perfect example of such an arrow prayer:
'Lord, he whom thou lovest is sick.')[4] It is the mediating of
presence which matters. We are much less sceptical than we
used to be about the way in which we communicate with one
another at the subconscious level. To intercede for another
person is to surround that person with a loving atmosphere; it
is as if we are providing an oxygen tent in which he is given the
space to cope more easily, and feel supported in his life-battles.
We may all have different ways of doing this. Some find it helpful to keep intercession lists, in the course of their prayers, with
periodic revision, so that each person may be remembered
systematically; others, less prone to such regularity of routine,
find it easier to have moments of loving attention at different
times in the day. We often say, 'I was only thinking about him,
and wondering . . . this morning,' and intercessory prayer
might well be described as giving our minds to people over a
period of time. Most of our ways of looking at prayer have been
too unimaginative and inflexible, and the more the complex
and hurried life of the twentieth century has impinged on
people, the less realistic has become the traditional framework
of morning and evening prayers. That is no cause for guilt: it
may well be that we are being liberated to enjoy richer
experiences.

What humiliates, looking back at one's attempts at prayer,
is the pretentiousness of it all. The elaborate categories which

were explained to me when I became a Christian – categories
of praise and thanksgiving, of meditation and intercession.
One dutifully tried to think oneself into gratitude and penit-
ence and all the rest. I have never quite thrown off the sense
of gloom and failure which hung over the whole attempt for
me – I felt like a mongol trying to learn Greek. Part of the
misery had to do with the talk of relationship with God.
I hoped for something not unlike a daily telephone conversation with God, and was hurt that he seemed undisposed to
chat.[5]

'The daily telephone conversation' which Monica Furlong
speaks of here may make prayer sound trivial, but the normal-
ity, the taking the reality for granted, the intimacy are all that
prayer should surely imply. However else we describe it, prayer
is relationship, that which keeps us close to the source of all our
caring. Just as in any close human relationship both partners
can come to see life and other people through the eyes of the
other, so the relationship which is prayer helps us to see and go
on seeing other people with and through his eyes. We shall
(dare I say it?) develop something of the sensitivity we see
Jesus display as he talked with the woman by the well, handled
his querulous disciples, saw right through to the loving heart of
the woman who anointed his feet. And we shall not only begin
to see other people as he would see them; we shall begin to see
him in them, come to reverence him in them, come to reverence
them. No one has expressed this truth, stemming from Jesus'
own parable of the sheep and the goats, better than Turgenev,
in a most moving piece of literature:

I saw myself, in dream, a youth, almost a boy, in a low-
pitched wooden church. The slim wax candles gleamed, spots
of red, before the old pictures of the saints.
   A ring of coloured light encircled each tiny flame. Dark
and dim it was in the church . . . But there stood before me
many people. All fair-haired, peasant heads. From time to
time they began swaying, falling, rising again, like the ripe

ears of wheat, when the wind of summer passes in slow undulation over them.

All at once some man came up from behind and stood beside me.

I did not turn towards him; but at once I felt that this man was Christ.

Emotion, curiosity, awe overmastered me suddenly. I made an effort . . . and looked at my neighbour.

A face like every one's, a face like all men's faces. The eyes looked a little upwards, quietly and intently. The lips closed, but not compressed; the upper lip, as it were, resting on the lower; a small beard parted in two. The hands folded and still. And the clothes on him like every one's.

'What sort of Christ is this?' I thought. 'Such an ordinary, ordinary man! It can't be!'

I turned away. But I had hardly turned my eyes away from this ordinary man when I felt again that it really was none other than Christ standing beside me.

Again I made an effort over myself . . . And again the same face, like all men's faces, the same everyday though unknown features.

And suddenly my heart sank, and I came to myself. Only then I realized that just such a face – a face like all men's faces – is the face of Christ.[6]

Such a reverence for the person, such a transfiguration of the ordinary; that is the heart of true pastoral care. It is also a major hope for our world which is rapidly becoming dehumanized.

Epilogue (or Prologue?)

A few years ago, a Scottish lady, we'll call her Mrs Campbell, went in search of her husband who'd left her because, as he said, he kept letting her down through drink. All she knew, through a postcard he'd sent her, was that he was somewhere in the Manchester area. It was a cold wet afternoon in early January when, after a rail journey from Glasgow, she stepped off what was then a number 48 bus, into a murky, traffic-crowded Manchester street. She'd never been out of Scotland before, she had a pound in her pocket, she had no bed for the night and no friend to whom she could turn. The bus-stop was just outside the church, a large, galleried Victorian edifice which, if you could look at it objectively, you'd say was rather ugly. But it was open, it was warm and the light of the Christmas crib was sufficient for our Scottish lady to see her way inside. Mrs Campbell sat down in the quiet of the church and pondered, leaving her considerable baggage under the pew. Presently Mrs Andrews, a member of the congregation and Mothers' Union, came in – not alas, to pray, though of course she wouldn't have dreamt of going away without – but in order to put a copy of *Readers' Digest* on the table – her monthly present for the rector, since she had been given *two* Christmas gift subscriptions. It was a strange subdued conversation which ensued when Mrs Andrews caught sight of Mrs Campbell – and poor Mrs Andrews never realized what she was in for when the innocent thought of the rector's *Readers' Digest* entered her head. For she found herself taking Mrs Campbell to her already over-crowded home for the night with her essential requisites, whilst she left her baggage under the pew, muttering, 'It'll be all right there.' They managed. But the next day, to ease the accommodation problem, Mrs Andrews asked a crippled lady from the church and her sister, living just across the road from the building, to see what they could do. It was sufficient simply to be asked; no more conditions were necessary. They gave Mrs Campbell the room they had, with an enormous double bed and 'Home Sweet Home' in Gothic lettering above the bed for good measure. The three of them got on so well that Mrs Campbell felt able to confide in them, and tell her little story, which was received with great sympathy and many unhelpful suggestions. Soon Mrs Campbell became attracted to the daily offices of the church; she would persist in standing when others were sitting and sitting when others were kneeling. No matter . . . and she soon had several people in the church doing detective work in and around the area, searching for her vagrant husband. It was ten days later when one or two members of the parish saw her, two days after she had given herself another three days in which to find her man. There she was, triumphantly striding along the busy street, her man (considerably smaller than she was) trotting at her side, obediently carrying the large suitcase.

That true story, from an ordinary Manchester parish, is such a glorious parable of what the church is. Mrs Campbell found the church open and warm, and she wouldn't have looked at it twice if it hadn't been. She came across ordinary people in an everyday situation spontaneously caring, in what (to the world at least) would be an extraordinary way. She was accepted, as herself – and with no strings attached, she was helped. No questions about her past life; no catechizing about her religious affiliations. And the result? Nothing will shake her now in her conviction that the church really is the Body of Christ, stretching out his arms to draw, to heal, to bring together, the place where we really *belong*. Obviously, Mrs Campbell's story doesn't represent the *end* of all our pastoral caring in the church; but it might be a beginning . . .

Notes and Suggestions for
Further Reading

Notes and Suggestions for Further Reading

Chapter 1

1. H. J. Clinebell Jr, *Basic Types of Pastoral Counselling*, Abingdon Press, New York and Nashville 1966, pp. 13f.
2. I John 4.19.
3. *The Oxford Book of Christian Verse*, Oxford University Press 1940, pp. 152f.
4. Jack Dominian, *Depression*, Fontana Books 1976.
5. Colin Murray Parkes, *Bereavement: Studies of Grief in Adult Life*, Penguin Books 1975.
6. Michael Hocking, *Church Times*, 14 March 1980.

There is perhaps no better example of the interweaving of insights from the fields of psychology and theology than that to be found in the collection of addresses by Harry Williams, *The True Wilderness*, Fontana Books 1976.

Chapter 2

1. A. H. Maslow, *Motivation and Personality*, Harper and Bros, New York 1970.
2. II Thess. 3.10.
3. Christine Smith, *Clouds got in my way*, Eyre Methuen 1981.

Readers may find it useful to consult: Anthony Storr, *The Integrity of the Personality*, Penguin Books 1960; Jack Dominian, *Cycles of Affirmation*, Darton, Longman and Todd 1975.

Chapter 3

1. W. A. Clebsch and C. R. Jaekle, *Pastoral Care in Historical Perspective*, Harper Torchbooks, New York 1967, p. 4.

2. Ibid., p. 6.
3. I Peter 3.15.
4. Luke 17.19.
5. Quoted by R. S. Lee, *Principles of Pastoral Counselling*, SPCK 1968, pp. 65f.
6. M. Buber, *Pointing the Way*, Routledge and Kegan Paul 1957, p. 54.
7. Dietrich Bonhoeffer, *Life Together*, SCM Press 1954, p. 75.
8. Laurens van der Post, *The Night of the New Moon*, Hogarth Press 1970, p. 154.
9. Ibid., p. 155.
10. Luke 22.42.
11. Mark 15.34.

Edgar N. Jackson, *The Role of Faith in the Process of Healing*, SCM Press 1981, is a difficult but rewarding book on the subject of healing; see also a useful collection of talks edited by Norman Autton, *From Fear to Faith: Studies in Suffering and Wholeness*, SPCK 1971. For more about logotherapy see Viktor Frankl, *The Doctor and the Soul*, Penguin Books 1973.

Chapter 4

1. Edward Albee, *The Zoo Story*, Penguin Books 1965, pp. 174f.
2. Iris Murdoch, 'The Idea of Perfection', in *The Sovereignty of Good*, Routledge and Kegan Paul 1970, pp. 43f.
3. Tony Lake, *Relationships*, Michael Joseph 1981, pp. 27–32.
4. George Herbert, 'Constancy', *Works of George Herbert*, ed. F. E. Hutchinson, Clarendon Press 1941, pp. 72f.
5. Michael Johnson, 'The Church's New Disenfranchised?', *Theology*, November 1981, p. 441.
6. Matt. 12.48–50.
7. Monica Furlong, *Divorce*, The Mothers' Union 1981, pp. 19f.
8. Jill Tweedie, *In the Name of Love*, Jonathan Cape 1979, p. 181.

Some will find Rosemary Haughton, *Love*, Penguin Books 1974, helpful on the subject of relationships, and Jack Dominian, *Marriage Relationship Today*, Mothers' Union 1974, is a useful summary of his views. Those views are found in a more recent and expanded version in his *Marriage, Faith and Love*, Darton, Longman and Todd 1981. Divorce is superbly well treated not only in Monica Furlong's personal statement, but also in Joseph Epstein, *Divorce*, Jonathan Cape 1975.

Chapter 5

1. Rollo May, *The Courage to Create*, Bantam Books, New York 1975, pp. 138f.
2. Published by Age Concern England, Mitcham, Surrey 1980. Their working-party report, *Claim to be Heard*, 1980, is equally useful.
3. Ronald Blythe, *The View in Winter*, Penguin Books 1981, p. 13.

Chapter 6

1. George Macleod, *Only One Way Left*, Iona Community 1954, pp. 115f.
2. Gordon Allport, *The Person in Psychology*, Beacon Press, Boston 1968, pp. 131f.

As background to this and the last chapter, readers may find it useful to read Jolande Jacobi, *Masks of the Soul*, Darton, Longman and Todd 1976.

Chapter 7

1. Charles Causley, 'Ten Types of Hospital Visiting', *Collected Poems 1951–1975*, Macmillan 1975, pp. 245–8.

Reades may be helped, as I have been, by Sylvia Poss, *Towards Death with Dignity*, Allen and Unwin 1981, and Lily Pincus, *Death and the Family*, Faber 1976.

Chapter 8

1. The movement is described in Roger Lloyd, *Adventure in Discipleship*, Longmans, Green 1953.
2. Dietrich Bonhoeffer, *Letters and Papers from Prison*, SCM Press 1971, p. 312.
3. John 16.22.
4. John 11.3.
5. Monica Furlong, *Travelling In*, Hodder and Stoughton 1971, p. 52.
6. Quoted in Victor Gollancz, *A Year of Grace*, Gollancz 1950, pp. 51f. from *Dream Tales and Prose Poems*, trs Constance Garnett, Heinemann.

A moving description of the resources of the pastoral carer's needs is to be found in the last chapter of Alastair Campbell, *Rediscovering Pastoral Care*, Darton, Longman and Todd 1981, but the whole book is essential reading for all of us.